CHALLENGES FOR THE 1990s FOR ARMS CONTROL AND INTERNATIONAL SECURITY

Committee on International Security and Arms Control

National Academy of Sciences

NATIONAL ACADEMY PRESS
Washington, D.C. 1989

The work that provided the basis for this volume was supported by funding from the Carnegie Corporation of New York, the W. Alton Jones Foundation, the John D. and Catherine T. MacArthur Foundation, and the Andrew W. Mellon Foundation.

Library of Congress Catalog Card Number 89-63431
International Standard Book Number 0-309-04084-1

Additional copies of this report are available from:

National Academy Press
2101 Constitution Avenue, NW
Washington, DC 20418

S008

Printed in the United States of America

Seminar Participants

R. James Woolsey,* Esq., Shea & Gardner; Under Secretary of the Navy, 1977–1979

Roald Sagdeev,* Director Emeritus, Institute of Space Research, Academy of Sciences of the USSR

Brig. General Roland Lajoie,* Director, U.S. On-Site Inspection Agency

Matthew Meselson,* Professor of Biochemistry and Molecular Biology, Harvard University

COMMITTEE ON INTERNATIONAL SECURITY AND ARMS CONTROL

Wolfgang K. H. Panofsky,* (*Chairman*), Director Emeritus, Stanford Linear Accelerator Center, Stanford University

Robert Axelrod, Arthur W. Bromage Professor of Political Science and Public Policy, University of Michigan

Paul M. Doty,* Department of Biochemistry and Molecular Biology, and Director Emeritus, Center for Science and International Affairs, Harvard University

Alexander H. Flax, President Emeritus, Institute for Defense Analyses; and Home Secretary, National Academy of Engineering

Richard L. Garwin, Science Adviser to the Director of Research, Thomas J. Watson Research Center, IBM Corporation

Marvin L. Goldberger,* Director, Institute for Advanced Study

David C. Jones, General (USAF, Ret.), Private Consultant

Spurgeon M. Keeny, Jr.,* President, Arms Control Association

Catherine M. Kelleher, Director, Center for International Security Studies, School of Public Affairs, University of Maryland

Joshua Lederberg, President, Rockefeller University

Claire Max, Associate Director, Institute of Geophysics and Planetary Physics, Lawrence Livermore National Laboratory

Michael May, Director Emeritus, Lawrence Livermore National Laboratory

---

*Seminar speaker.

Foreword

Since its creation in 1863, the National Academy of Sciences has undertaken many studies and activities relating to matters of national security, and currently several committees of the National Research Council advise branches of the military on questions of scientific research. Other Academy committees have studied such topics as nuclear winter and the contribution of behavioral and social sciences to the prevention of nuclear war.

The Committee on International Security and Arms Control (CISAC) reflects the Academy's deep interest in international security and the potential of arms control to reduce the threat of nuclear and conventional war. Its members have been deeply involved in many aspects of military technology and arms control. They have advised several presidents and served in senior governmental posts; they have been involved with important arms control negotiations; they have thought long and hard about national security issues.

CISAC has pursued a number of activities in response to its broad charter. Twice each year it meets with its counterparts from the Soviet Academy of Sciences to explore problems of international security and arms control. In response to the widely expressed interest of Academy members in learning more about issues and opportunities in arms control, it has convened a number of meetings and sessions on arms control specifically for them. In the spring of 1984 CISAC conducted a major tutorial for over 200 Academy members. The background materials for that tutorial resulted in the book *Nuclear Arms Control: Background and Issues*, published in 1985. CISAC conducted a seminar on strategic defense in 1985 and cosponsored one the following year on crisis management that resulted in the short publication *Crisis Management in the Nuclear Age*.

In the spring of 1987 CISAC presented a seminar for the Academy audience that explored the implications of the proposals for very deep cuts in strategic nuclear arsenals that had been discussed by President Reagan and General Secretary Gorbachev at the Reykjavik summit in 1986. That seminar was captured in a small publication entitled *Reykjavik and Beyond: Deep Reductions in Strategic Nuclear Arsenals and the Future Direction of Arms Control.*

In the spring of 1989 CISAC held its fifth seminar for the membership of the National Academy of Sciences on challenges for the 1990s for arms control and international security. The initial rationale for these seminars—that the scientific community generally and the National Academy of Sciences specifically are an important resource to give independent counsel to the government and the public on vital issues that have a major scientific component—remains as valid today as it has ever been. Issues of international security and arms control are prominent in this category, and so I am pleased to present this next in what has become a continuing series of Academy publications of the proceedings of this important series of CISAC-sponsored seminars. The committee hopes to help inform a wider Academy and public audience through these publications.

I would like to express my great appreciation to the chairman, members, and staff of CISAC, some of whom contributed to this volume and all of whom dedicate much time and effort to the activities of the committee. I believe the committee continues to learn a great deal in the course of its work, and I hope that others will judge that work, including this volume, to be useful in their own effort to understand the contribution of arms control to international security.

Frank Press, *President*
National Academy of Sciences

Contents

CONTENTS

1

Challenges for International Security in the 1990s

R. James Woolsey

When Dr. Press called me a while back to make these remarks tonight, and I was deeply honored to be invited, he was gentle in his polite way, but his underlying message was, "Keep it general, Woolsey, and do not try to lecture all these distinguished scientists, the way you are wont to from time to time, on the virtues of small mobile ICBMs and 30 PSI hard mobile launchers and the like."

This subtle admonition not to lecture, lawyer-like, recalled an experience I had when I was a lieutenant in the Army, working in the Office of the Secretary of Defense for Alain Enthoven, in Systems Analysis, back at the end of the 1960s. My boss was an Air Force colonel, a very able man with a great deal of technical training and scientific background. We were working on intelligence issues, working with another staff, part of the intelligence community, that was supposed to produce an interagency paper for us to review and take to a meeting on Monday.

Late Friday afternoon he said, "Jim, do you want to come in and help me work on this tomorrow, because we have to get this paper ready?" I said, "Arch"—Systems Analysis was an informal place and lieutenants called colonels by their first name—"I am glad to come work all weekend, no problem, but the other staff is going to put the paper together. We are

1

just supposed to read it and go to the meeting on Monday. Why are we writing our own?"

He said, "Well, you know it is not going to be any good. We really have to do the work for everybody." I said, "Well, I am glad to do it, but why do you think it is not going to be any good?" He said, "You know that staff out there; it is a bunch of lawyers."

I pulled a slightly long face, having just been notified that week that I had actually passed the bar and being moderately proud of that modest achievement. He realized that he had said something—he was a kind man, too, just like Frank Press. And so he said, "Oh, Jim, I'm sorry. I don't mean like you. I mean real lawyers."

This morning's newspaper was remarkable. Your colleague of tomorrow, Roald Sagdeev, as well as a fascinating economist, Mr. Smiliov, and, of course, most remarkably, Sakharov himself, have been elected to the Congress of People's Deputies—Sakharov after demonstrations in the streets in Moscow in his support.

One hundred fifty thousand students massed in Beijing in Tiananmen Square, chanting for democracy and liberty with signs in English and Chinese, singing the Internationale, "Arise ye prisoners of starvation, arise ye wretched of the earth." Portraits of Marx, Engels, Lenin, and Stalin have long been down on Tiananmen Square—only Mao is left at one end—and on the other end of the Square, overlooking this scene, is another portrait: Colonel Sanders. The largest Kentucky fried chicken restaurant in the world is now on Tiananmen Square. So as the leadership of communist China walks out of the funeral which they are attending there—the memorial service—past tens of thousands of students chanting slogans that would have been familiar to Thomas Jefferson, they are overseen by the founder of their regime and by the Kentucky colonel. The times are quite remarkable.

It seems to me that the overall issue we have to assess in this circumstance—particularly given your program for tomorrow and the title of your organization, the Committee on International Security and Arms Control—is really what the relationship is in this time and in these circumstances between international security and arms control.

There is an old parlor game in which one is given the answer and is supposed to invent the question. For example, "9W." What is the question to which that might be the answer? "Do you spell it with a V, Mr. Wagner?" If the answer is arms control, what is the question?

3

It seems to me that one problem we have had over the course of the last 20 years or so of negotiating with the Soviets on, first, strategic, and, if you count MBFR—and I suppose you should—conventional arms control, is the assumption on, more or less, the left-hand side of the political spectrum, that arms control is The Answer (capital T, capital A) and, on the right-hand side of the political spectrum, that it is The Problem (capital T, capital P).

In fact, in these days and times I really do not think it is either one, at least not with capital letters. I think the Joint Chiefs' formulation some years ago about SALT II, "modest but useful," is about right and that we are moving into a period in which we could—with a little bit of luck and some sensible planning on our own part and the continuation of Mr. Gorbachev's reforms in the Soviet Union—produce some reasonably modest, useful arms control agreements, both on strategic and on conventional forces.

But I would view them more as a lubricant for the evolution of stable and sensible national security policies on our part, and in the East as well, rather than as some overriding or overweening objective—not an Answer (capital A).

I am speaking of an evolution in a general direction toward strategic and conventional force stability, and when one talks that way—often with our Soviet friends—one gets the answer, "But what is your objective? What is your end point? How do you know what you are trying to do unless you know exactly where it is you are trying to go? Do you not believe that a nonnuclear world is what we should be trying for? What steps are you taking in order to get there?"

In talking with them I am often reminded of a wonderful exchange in the Holmes-Lasky letters between Justice Oliver Wendell Holmes, Jr., and the British socialist, Harold Lasky. Lasky, in his continental style and as part of his continental tradition—reaching, really, back to Plato, and in its notion of a general, overall approach toward philosophical problems back through Hegel, Kant, Marx, Descartes—developed a very elaborate argument from first principles of something that he wanted to convince Holmes of.

Holmes wrote back a one-sentence letter: "My dear Lasky, man was born to formulate general propositions, and none of them was ever worth a damn. Yours, Holmes."

You could not have a clearer confrontation between the tradition of—

reaching, really, back to Aristotle—pragmatism and the empiricism of Mills, Locke, Hume, Will James, and Holmes and the tradition of seeking refuge in an overriding principle.

And that, in part, is what is going on when we and our friends—sometimes our allied friends such as the French, but certainly in our discussions with the Soviets—end up haggling with one another about whether or not you can make progress without a single overriding objective. Those of us in the pragmatic tradition tend to think it is all right if you can get the herd roughly headed west and see if you cannot make some progress (sort of like the Lewis and Clark expedition); whereas the Soviet perspective is often far more one of trying to formulate a general, overreaching concept, all-embracing—and not just the Soviets but in many ways the continental Europeans as well. It is an attitude about progress that works in a very different way, very much the way Holmes and Lasky clashed. Isaiah Berlin calls it the difference between "hedgehogs" (who "know one big thing") and "foxes" (who "know many things").

Now I consider myself very much in the Holmes, the fox, tradition on this dispute. I have very rarely—and this will not surprise you for a lawyer—met a general proposition of which I was not at least partially skeptical. I have a feeling that the demonstrations in Tiananmen Square and the demonstrations on behalf of Sakharov in the streets of Moscow a short time back—which had something to do, I believe, with his election yesterday—may indicate some development along these more pragmatic lines of thinking in the East as well as in the West. We do not know where all of this is going on their side. It may be quite hopeful, but it may not work out.

After all, if one wants to look for historical comparisons—for Russia, let us say—there was another nation, at one time a very powerful nation, that stood on the frontiers of Europe, and had an extremely autocratic state and church culture, the church as part of the state. It saw itself as the bulwark against Islam and protector of Europe and came into the mid-twentieth century after a period as a monarchy and as a totalitarian power, albeit a small one. I am speaking of Spain.

It is less than a long generation from totalitarianism to autocracy to democracy in Spain. If we want to look for a positive historical model, Spain might be it. And in spite of its very different historical experience, there are some interesting parallels between Russia and Spain, drawn very well, I would say, by Jim Billington in his wonderful work, *The Icon and the Axe.*

If we want to be optimistic about where the Russian empire might go, we might think of Spain. If we want to be pessimistic, we will look back on the four or five or six attempts at reform in the Russian empire before the coming of the communist revolution, and the couple or so afterward, and remember that the reforms of Peter the Great and Alexander II and, in the early twentieth century, the reforms by Stolypin under Nicholas II, the reforms at the end of Lenin's life, the New Economic Policy (NEP), the political reforms under Khrushchev have all in one way been followed by—sometimes accompanied by—a period of repression and retrogression.

In my pessimistic moments I think of Gorbachev as a modern-day Alexander II. The optimistic young czar who came to power in 1855 in the aftermath of the Crimean War, who freed the serfs, who held forth to the world and to Russia as a whole a great dream of liberalization, whose reforms began to slow over the years as the aristocracy, the army, the church, and the structural powers in Russia thwarted his efforts—until he was finally assassinated.

Are we looking toward a Spain or toward a rerun of Alexander II? I do not know. What I do believe is that for a substantial period of time some of the old verities of maintaining deterrence—deterrence with a nuclear component to it—and collective security with allies such as NATO and Japan are going to have to be a centerpiece of our policy in dealing with the Soviet Union.

Nuclear weapons cannot be "disinvented" anyway. One may, in Sam Nunn's phrase, be able to evolve toward a "less nuclear world." I think that is plausible with survivable nuclear forces, forces that are well controlled (by command and communications), safe and secure against terrorism and accidents. I do not believe that reducing numbers is the main thing, although it may be, in some circumstances, moderately useful. But I think our long-run objective ought, really, to be boredom with nuclear weapons—not abolition, not a crusade.

Arms control, I think, has a role in that evolution. First of all, it has to follow the Hippocratic oath, primum non nocere; first of all, do no harm. Proposals such as those that were instituted at the end of 1985 and are still formally the position of the U.S. Government, such as a ban on mobile

ICBMs, to me, violate this arms control Hippocratic oath, since I think mobiles are the best way—not the only way, but the best way—to achieve survivable land-based forces for the long run.

It seems to me that what arms control may help accomplish is a shift toward more survivable and safer systems. There is room for disagreement about how to do this. I tend to focus on offensive forces and think about things like mobility. Others concentrate more on SDI. But if one stays within the framework of the START agreement as it is—perhaps three-quarters to seven-eighths negotiated—I believe that an agreement with the Soviet Union within the next year or two is a reasonable prospect. It is something that can set a framework for us to continue to maintain a survivable and, hopefully, more boring nuclear deterrent as the years roll on and we see what develops in this relationship with the East, whether they take the path of modern Spain or of Russia under Alexander II.

Conventional forces of some strength and numbers I believe we are going to need for a substantial number of years—partly for reasons unrelated to the Soviet Union, having to do with renegade states such as Libya and the rest. I think that our conventional deterrent in Europe and the structure of NATO is, if we are lucky, going to last many more years and will, in part, depend in some degree on reliance on a nuclear deterrent, including some types of nuclear weapons maintained in Europe.

One may be able to decrease their numbers and radically reduce the numbers of nuclear artillery shells, for example, but I believe some type of nuclear capability is the glue that holds the alliance together. The commitment of the American nuclear shield is going to be essential.

I was at a conference a few years ago in which the evolution away from nuclear and toward conventional deterrence was the main theme. A French participant more or less stopped the show by standing up and saying, "I have heard at this conference much talk of conventional deterrence. I have only one thing to say. The history of the nation-state in Europe for the last millennium teaches one and only one lesson with absolute clarity: Conventional deterrence does not work."

It is a reasonable thought and no one had a very good answer, in spite of a great deal of arm waving about replacing nuclear with conventional deterrence that had taken place up until that time.

Equal numbers of conventional forces on each side are no guarantee of stability, however. Our current proposals to the Soviets, ones which they have come very close to matching on tanks and armored troop carriers and artillery, would suggest an evolution toward equal numbers at a level slightly (5 to 15 percent) below the current NATO levels. That is certainly better than what we have now, but it is no guarantee—as my French friend would suggest—of any long-term stability.

The Germans, after all, attacked and won, outnumbered significantly in both men and in armor, both against France and against Russia in 1940 and 1941. Within a two-hour drive of where we are now, there are no fewer than eight battlefields on which Stonewall Jackson won, outnumbered two to one. Indeed, Stonewall Jackson never even considered it interesting until he was outnumbered two to one.

Throughout military history it has been possible and plausible for able commanders to concentrate their forces, break through, destroy the will of their opponents, and succeed, even when outnumbered. So, equal numbers across the front in Europe, negotiated as part of an arms control agreement or otherwise, are not going to do the job without something else.

What is going to be necessary is reducing the ability for a blitzkrieg to be conducted effectively. The cuts that Gorbachev announced in December, if they are taken in modern and effective and forward-deployed forces—as we can all hope and, I think, should expect they will be—will certainly be a help to this end. But a good deal more is going to need to be done in order to introduce some degree of stability into the conventional balance. I think, for many, many years, stability is going to require some degree of nuclear deterrence in order to ensure that the peace is kept— regardless of the degree of reform in the Soviet Union.

With the right type of changes on the Soviet side and on our side, however, I think we can expect some substantial changes in the structure of those forces deployed in Europe—perhaps a rather greater reliance on reserves—both in Europe for the Europeans and in the United States for ourselves. That, in my mind, is the best way to try to save money in the defense budget, not to try to destroy the modernization of our forces and not to drag down the readiness across the board, as was done in the 1970s in the aftermath of Vietnam.

It will require, both for our allies and ourselves, some rather major restructuring of the way our reserves work. But to me that is far and away the most reasonable approach—far more so than most of the alternatives—and it will take time. Almost any effort to try to save substantial amounts of money out of the defense budget within the next year or two as a result of arms control agreements or restructuring in response to Gorbachev or anything else are going to end up severely undercutting our military position, I believe. But in time I think substantial amounts can be saved if a major shift from active to reserve forces is handled in the proper way.

I want to finish up by saying something about what I think is going to be, in many ways, the major challenge for international security for all of us, if we are able to see a continued positive evolution in the Soviet Union, maintain our own defenses prudently—as I have suggested—and have, perhaps, some framework-setting arms control agreements of the sort that we are pointing toward in START and in the CFE (Conventional Forces in Europe) talks, as both sides have made their proposals in Vienna.

The area I want to mention briefly is environment and energy use, because it affects our international security directly. Dependence—for us and even more for our European allies and the Japanese—on oil, particularly from the Middle East, continues to be destabilizing. The Middle East is unstable enough as a world hot spot for religious and nationalistic rivalries without adding to it the West's dependence upon it for energy.

It is and I think it remains the most troubling part of the world from the point of view of its importance, its instability, and the possibility of both the United States and the Soviet Union feeling they have vital interests there and getting involved in some sort of hostilities in support of their friends and allies.

I do not have to tell this audience that, of course, hydrocarbon burning is a major part of the global warming problem as well. We are losing in deforestation—which is also a major contributor—roughly an area the size of Austria in forests a year.

If present emission trends continue for hydrocarbons, according to some recent work by Jessica Tuchman Matthews, with no offsetting cooling mechanism—such as increased clouds and the like—you can take your pick, but current models put the temperature increase by the early 2030s (which is in the lifetime of today's college students) as an increase of between 3 and 8 degrees Fahrenheit. The earth has not been that hot for 2 million years, since before the beginning of homo sapiens.

Then let me share with you some recent energy statistics from the Rocky Mountain Institute.

In energy use we have gone—ourselves, as a nation—from being grotesque gluttons to merely being fulsome gourmands. From 1977 to 1985 we made some progress. We had about a 5 percent annual improvement in our productivity in oil product use, mainly from a five-mile-per-gallon improvement in automobile efficiency.

We saved oil then about 80 percent faster than we needed to in order to compensate both for our economic growth and for declining domestic production, and we cut our imports in half. That has turned around in the last few years. The amount of crude oil that we wasted in 1986 alone by rolling back the automobile efficiency standards equaled the entire U.S. previous year's imports from the Persian Gulf. It also equals, just about, our annual expected output from the Arctic National Wildlife Refuge, should we tap it.

Our imports would plummet if we had only Japanese and European mileage standards for our automobiles. If you move from oil to energy as a whole, in the last decade, again, we have gone from being complete gluttons merely to being bad gourmands. We have increased our available energy by seven times as much using conservation, seven times as much as we have from all net energy increases, and due to the improvements we have brought about since the first oil shock in 1973, our annual energy bill in this country is roughly $430 billion instead of $580 billion, saving $150 billion a year. As Everett Dirksen used to say, "$150 billion here, $150 billion there, before you know it, it adds up to real money."

But, again, if we just had European and Japanese energy efficiency today, we would be saving approximately another $200 billion on our energy bill.

Can we make these types of changes, the types of investments necessary to do something about our energy gluttony and the negative contributions we are making to the world's environmental crises? Or are we stopped by massive defense spending, by our "imperial overreach"?

In my judgment, applying that concept to the United States is among the weakest of arguments affecting public policy that has been put forward in the public arena from a respected academic within the last several years. The U.S. defense budget today is about half the GNP share that it was during the Kennedy Administration—about 5 percent rather than 10 percent of the gross national product (GNP).

We spend on health care about double what we spend on defense, and about half of health care is hospitals. So the defense budget is roughly equivalent to what we spend on hospitals in the United States today. Those, on the average, are operating at 60 percent of capacity.

Have we otherwise collapsed in our ability to make these changes, these investments, that are needed because of some sharp decline in our GNP since the late 1940s and early 1950s by some inability to produce industrial goods compared with the rest of the world?

Such allegations are, in my judgment, simply wrong. Charles Wolff of Rand has pointed out that the United States' share of world GNP has been a couple of percentage points—give or take a percent—under 25 percent (nearly a quarter of the world's GNP) at the turn of the century, in the late 1930s, in the 1960s, and today, and it is projected to be that around the end of the century.

When it was not just under a quarter of the world's GNP was in the late 1940s. But in the late 1940s we had just won World War II. Our allies— the Soviet Union, China, and England—were devastated from the victory. Our enemies were devastated from our military actions. As Shakespeare said, in Julius Caesar, "We bestrode the world like a colossus." We had nearly half the world's GNP.

Any assumption that the United States was destined, for any period of time, to dominate the world's economy, with our tiny share of the world's population, to the tune of nearly half of the world's GNP, and that any decline from those days of the late 1940s is evidence of some type of decline in our civilization, I would submit, is simply ridiculous.

Turning to some figures from Professor Joseph Nye of Harvard, the United States' share of world industrial output was 32 percent in 1938. Has it declined? Yes, by 1 percent. It is 31 percent today. Our share of the world output of high technology over the last 15 years, since the early 1970s, has vacillated between 24 and 25 percent.

Yes, we have lost in some key areas, in electronics, particularly in terms of manufacturing capability, partially because some of our friends in Asia have learned manufacturing and quality control techniques that were invented here and that we forgot. But in terms of some overall share, decline of our influence in the world compared with any other part of the twentieth century, except the days immediately following World War II, is very hard to find.

The real problem, according to a superb article by Francis Bator in the most recent *Foreign Affairs* quarterly, is that we are eating our seed corn.

We invested, as a nation, between 8 and 10 percent of our GNP in the 1950s, in the 1960s, and in the 1970s. In the 1980s, in the last eight years, it has dropped to 2 percent. We are investing approximately one-quarter of what we did in the three previous decades. Personal consumption has skyrocketed. In personal consumption—I am not talking about government spending—this richest nation on earth consumes a staggering two-thirds of its GNP.

There is nothing inherently wrong, Bator points out, with borrowing or with deficits if you are wisely investing what you are borrowing. Senator Pat Moynihan put it, as I think is often the case, exactly right. What has happened in the last decade is that we have borrowed a trillion (now it is a trillion-and-a-half) dollars from Japan and had a party. U.S. personal consumption is so high that minor shifts in it dwarf everything else.

Let us undertake a hypothetical thought experiment: Could we do something for the poor in the United States by making substantial cuts in defense? Absolutely. Again, using Bator's figures, if you hold defense to the share of GNP that is its 30-year low, 4.8 percent, we would cut defense by $39 billion this year. Transfer that to the poor, which is about 13 percent of the country, and you could increase an average poor family's consumption by over 50 percent, from a little over $8,000 a year to $12,500. Not a bad move, you say.

On the other hand, that kind of cut in defense might—to put it mildly—create some problems for national security. Are there other possibilities?

Alternatively, you might try brown bagging once a week or so. Let me explain what I mean. According to Bator's figures, a reduction in consumption from today's level for an average family of between three and four Americans of about $500 per year is a reduction from $44,600 (which is what we, the nonpoor, consume on the average per family today), down to $44,100. By the early 1990s, say 1993, this would do the following: It would make it possible to increase the consumption of all the poor in the United States by over 50 percent (the figure I gave earlier); it would keep the defense budget stable, in real terms, thereby holding on to what we may need for international security; and we would have enough left over to quadruple our national investment rate from 2 up to 8 percent or so, the way we talked about a minute ago. This could be done with these several years of foregone increases in consumption and an actual decrease in consumption down to a consumption level that is $500 per family below today. This is roughly $10 a week for a nonpoor family below today's consumption level, which could be saved by brown bagging it roughly once or twice a week, or maybe foregoing a movie plus popcorn—a small popcorn at today's movie popcorn prices.

Even small changes in our consumption are changes in such a huge base that many, many things—energy savings and others—become possible, if we will but make them.

Are there continuing international security problems? Yes. Can we deal with them with a stable, even declining, defense budget if we manage that transition? Well, I think so, but it is going to take care and gradualism and planning and sensible reductions and changes in our own policy. Arms control can help in this. But if you really want to do something about the other problems that are looming—environmental damage, energy, and the rest—there are a variety of solutions, but probably the simplest and the best for us as a nation is simply to determine that we are going to consume slightly less than we do now.

It can be said, as Bator suggests, that the American people will not put up with that; that we cannot confront them with the need to pay slightly higher gasoline taxes or any other steps that would be required in order to reallocate resources away from consumption and toward investment for these other needs.

If we do not urge it, what we resemble is a physician who sees an important patient with a serious degenerative disease and decides that he has to choose between letting the disease run its course and major surgery, even though a modest diet would solve the problem. And if you ask him—ask us—"Why don't you recommend a modest diet?" the answer is, "Those people do not like to diet. They will never do it."

2

Introductory Remarks: From INF to New Agreements

Wolfgang K. H. Panofsky

Ational security has many aspects, of which military preparedness is only one. In previous seminars we emphasized this diversity by including such topics as offensive versus defensive strategic armaments, the management of international crises, as well as specific discussion of arms control issues.

Since our last seminar two years ago, the world has changed drastically in respect to national security affairs. The INF Treaty has been signed and ratified. What we call the mandate conference determining the charge for the Conventional Forces in Europe talks has been concluded. The Strategic Arms Reduction Talks (START) have progressed, but concluding that treaty has eluded the Reagan Administration.

Above all, there has been a drastic change in the climate in which future arms control will operate. There has been an increased weariness in pursuing war as a means of resolving conflicts. The Iran-Iraq war has been terminated by an uneasy truce. Soviet troops have left Afghanistan. The Vietnamese are leaving Cambodia, and Cubans are leaving Angola. The Contras are no longer a significant force in Nicaragua. The two Koreas are exploring contacts leading to communication and, maybe, a long time hence, unification. A China-Soviet summit is in view, after a

30-year lapse. Above all, the Soviets have announced unilateral moves, particularly with respect to Europe, which promise to lessen greatly the asymmetry with respect to both conventional and nuclear weapons in that most heavily armed region of the world.

All these factors signal moves away from conflict. But there are other, less favorable trends. Religious fundamentalism is on the increase. Terrorism and the drug traffic remain elusive of increased control measures.

Security of the world can no longer be described as a bipolar issue—as it has been simplistically by some—that is, dominated by the United States versus Soviet confrontation. National security no longer rests exclusively, or even primarily, on military might. In fact, during the last years it has become increasingly clear that the vastly excessive military weaponry of the United States and the Soviet Union is to some extent a burden rather than an asset. Economic strength and societal vitality may be more determinative to real security than military power.

The military losers of World War II have become the economic leaders of today. In this respect the growing strength of the Asiatic nations, in particular Japan, makes it clear that the age of world dominance by the United States and the Soviet Union is fading. The nations of the world are all struggling internally, by a variety of means and to varying degrees, to achieve an acceptable balance among social equity, productivity, and preservation of the earth's resources.

All this has, happily, tended to submerge the strictly military aspects of security. Yet military forces, in particular the nuclear deterrent, can be given at least some of the credit for having prevented all-out conflict for four decades. The maintenance of a stable, peaceful relationship among several nations intertwines military and political factors.

It is against this context that we would like to examine today, in this seminar, what should follow the INF Treaty in aiding the true national security of the United States, by reducing the dangers and burdens of arms and enhancing stability among the nations of the world.

The new Administration, similar to many previous ones, will have to make many decisions in the national security area which are a balance of risks. Neither increased arms nor increased arms control will ever be without perceived benefits or without costs and risks. We are hearing many voices today urging the Bush Administration to go slowly on arms control, because, indeed, wrong moves can be made in the name of reducing arms. But wrong moves can also be made, and frequently have

TABLE 1   The Number of Launchers and Bombers in the U.S. and Soviet Strategic Forces

Type	Present Inventories		START Proposed
	U.S.	USSR	
Total delivery vehicles	2,002	2,503	1,600
Heavy bombers	362	175	
BM total	1,640	2,328	
ICBM	1,000	1,386 (308 heavy)	(154 heavy)
SLBM	640	942	
Total throw weight of BMs			<50% of Soviet level "at reference time"

been made, in increasing arms. I would reject firmly the assumption underlying much of the go-slow counsel that risks in arms control are unacceptable, while risks in increased armaments are to be expected and condoned.

It is in this spirit that I would like to address the different moves which I envisage for the years to come.

First, there is START. The basic outline of that treaty is in place. Contrary to its public image, START will neither cut the total number of nuclear strategic delivery vehicles in half nor will it reduce the number of nuclear weapons of intercontinental range by that amount. The START draft treaty, as it stood by the end of last year, falls significantly short of that goal.

I will present two tables that will give an overview of the current inventory. Table 1 indicates the number of launchers—ICBMs and SLBMs—and bombers of the United States and the Soviet Union. The proposed START agreement is that the total number of delivery vehicles shall be reduced to 1,600, not by a factor of two. In addition to that, the total throw weight of ballistic missiles—that means the total amount of weight which can be thrown from one nation to the other—is to be reduced by a factor

TABLE 2   The Number of Warheads in the U.S. and Soviet
Strategic Forces

| Type | Present Inventories | | | | START Proposed |
| | U.S. | | USSR | | |
	SALT Counting Rules	START Counting Rules	SALT Counting Rules	START Counting Rules	
Total warheads	14,637	9,789[a]/ 10,585[b]	11,694	10,595[a]/ 10,455[b]	6,000[c]
Heavy bombers	5,608	1,784[a]/ 2,580[b]	1,620	805[a]/ 665[b]	1,100[b]
BM total	9,029	8,005	10,074	9,790	4,900
ICBM	2,373	2,373	6,412	6,412	3,000–3,300[a]
SLBM	6,656	5,632	3,662	3,378	3,300[b]
SLCM					400 Nuclear[b] 600 Nonnuclear[b]

NOTE: Numbers of warheads are agreed upon values unless otherwise noted.

[a]U.S. counting rules or U.S. position.
[b]Soviet counting rules or Soviet position.
[c]Under START counting rules actual warhead counts would be 20 to 30 percent larger.

of two at reference time. There is still disagreement on what that reference time is to be. There is a separate agreement that the 308 very heavy ballistic missiles, the SS-18s, that the Soviets have are to be reduced by half.

Table 2 displays a much more complex situation—namely, the number of warheads. As far as the number of warheads is concerned, it depends on how you count them. There are what we call the SALT counting rules and new counting rules at START. Under the new counting rules at

START, the same inventory counts at considerably lower numbers than it did under SALT. I will not go into detail here, only to point out that there are still some residual disagreements about how the load of warheads carried by heavy bombers is supposed to be counted. Note *a* in Table 2 indicates the U.S. positions and note *b* indicates the Soviet positions at the end of 1988. You will notice, in general, that the U.S. position tends to give a lower count of warheads.

The agreement is to reduce the total number of warheads to 6,000, however, using the START counting rules. Therefore, the actual ratio of reductions being proposed is something like a 40 percent reduction, not a 50 percent reduction.

In addition to these differences, there are disagreements about what we call sublimits. There is an agreement for the total number of ballistic missiles. The United States wishes to put a sublimit on the ICBMs, but none on the SLBMs, and since the Soviets have more ICBMs than SLBMs, naturally that is not something which the Soviets would accept. The Soviets are taking the "both or neither" position—namely, either to have a sublimit on SLBMs (on which we have more warheads than the Soviets) or none at all. So that is still a disagreed item, even though the bottom line of the number of ballistic missiles is agreed to.

To summarize, we have agreed on two warhead totals, with some disagreement on counting rules and on sublimits.

In addition to that, however, there are three major disagreements between the United States and the Soviet Union: the matters of mobile strategic ballistic missiles, sea-launched cruise missiles (SLCMs), and the linkage of START to constraints on the Strategic Defense Initiative (SDI). Let me briefly comment on each of these.

The current U.S. position is to prohibit mobile ballistic missiles unless verification problems can be resolved. That is the official phraseology. The Soviet position is to permit limited numbers of such missiles. Note that currently the Soviet Union has deployed the mobile SS-25 and SS-24, while the United States has not fielded any mobile ICBMs. A mobile version of the small Midgetman missile is being designed, but its approval for final development remains in doubt. The Air Force is proposing a mobile version of the MX; again, its final approval is at present in the political process.

In brief, the arguments against mobile missiles are: (1) their numbers cannot be verified with the same degree of precision as those of fixed land-based missiles and (2) the deployment of mobile ICBMs gives the Soviet Union a strategic advantage, since that country has a larger land area in which such missiles can operate. In contrast, public opinion would restrict the operation of mobile ICBMs in the United States to federally owned land.

An argument for mobile missiles is that they are more survivable against preemptive attack than are fixed land-based missiles, and they are therefore more suitable to serve as a deterrent, i.e., as second-strike weapons. Stability is enhanced if the survivability of the strategic forces of both nations is improved. So long as the Soviet Union continues to deploy a much smaller fraction of its strategic forces in submarines and strategic bombers, overall strategic stability would be enhanced if land-based mobile missiles were permitted.

The issue could easily be resolved at START by permitting the Soviets and the United States to retain limited numbers of mobile missiles. Since the number is small, the verification issue is minimal. The United States can then unilaterally decide whether deployment of such systems is worth the cost.

The second open issue is the matter of sea-launched cruise missiles. Here, in the 1987 Washington summit, Gorbachev and Reagan jointly declared that these missiles should be brought under a separate limit, but subsequent negotiations failed to reach agreement on just what is to be controlled and how such control is to be verified.

The Soviet position is that there shall be 400 nuclear SLCMs and 600 nonnuclear SLCMs. The U.S. position is that, for the time being, there shall be no numerical limit at all, but that there simply shall be a unilateral declaration of intent, stating the level of SLCM deployment that is supposed to go forward, but without any specific means of verification.

This matter has been studied extensively. Time does not permit me to discuss the technical nature of this complex issue. Sea-launched cruise missiles can be deployed with either conventional or lighter nuclear warheads and guidance packages of diverse weight. Their range is largely dependent on how their payload is divided among fuel, guidance, and weapons. Thus, controls on nuclear strategic SLCMs are inexorably linked with controls on conventionally armed shorter-range systems. Once the control regime has been decided upon, there are substantial verification issues to ensure compliance.

I would maintain that verification, although difficult and intrusive, can be achieved to meet reasonable standards for any of the regimes for limiting either nuclear or conventionally armed SLCMs.

Verification is, in fact, not the real issue. In actuality internal disagreements within the United States, and possibly also within the Soviet Union, as to the desired reach of control are impeding agreement. The dominant issue is the value that each navy places on retaining conventionally armed long-range SLCMs. The United States has a greater dependence on naval forces to maintain its supply lines to Europe and other national security objectives. This mission is greatly assisted by short-range conventional SLCMs, but long-range SLCMs are less relevant. Again, these matters should be resolvable.

Once such agreement is reached, the verification issues are, I believe, tractable, considering the willingness demonstrated in INF to accept intrusive inspection, about which we will hear more later in this program. The U.S. position, the 1987 summit declaration notwithstanding, in essence removes consideration of any SLCM limits from the current START framework. This deferral may be convenient but in my view is very undesirable. While the number of nuclear-armed SLCMs that would evolve during the next years is relatively small compared with the total number of strategic weapons now deployed, the lack of any nuclear SLCM limit would further compromise the definite ceiling on strategic delivery systems imposed by START. While the long flight times of SLCMs make them relatively unsuitable as first-strike weapons (and therefore the limited deployment would not be very destabilizing to the strategic balance in itself), they can contribute to the counterforce potential in connection with other systems.

Moreover, I consider the evolution of nuclear SLCMs to be highly undesirable, in the long run, both to the interests of arms control and to the security interests of the United States. The Soviet Union has a much smaller concentration of important military and industrial facilities near its coast. Therefore, the U.S. installations, in particular command and control centers, are much more vulnerable to SLCM attack than those of the Soviet Union. Therefore, if the SLCM dilemma is not resolved, in the long run, the United States will be the loser.

If the SLCM dilemma is not going to destroy the START agreement entirely, it must either be resolved at START or deferred. I would very much prefer the former, but I do not minimize the difficulties involved.

That leaves us with the linkage of START to SDI. The Soviet position is that the United States should obligate itself to abide by the 1972 ABM Treaty, "as signed," for a period of 10 years and as a precondition to Soviet willingness to go forward with the START treaty. After those 10 years, the ABM Treaty should remain in force for an unlimited duration. The United States has been unwilling, under the Reagan Administration, to accept the "as signed" formulation, since it would generally be interpreted to contradict the legal position promoted by the Reagan Administration in support of the so-called broad interpretation of the ABM Treaty, which permits unfettered development and testing of space weapons.

In my view the Soviet position is reasonable and acceptable, and recent events have reinforced that conclusion. Over the next 10 years, considering both technical practicalities and the realities of the budget, a sensibly managed U.S. research and development program on ballistic missile defense can well be carried out within the traditional interpretation of the ABM Treaty. Moreover, the Congress has been unwilling, and is expected to remain unwilling, to authorize test programs that would contradict the narrow interpretation.

Most important, the U.S. position, in its raw form, establishes a basic violation of the ABM Treaty, which is the only treaty now in force in the field of strategic arms, as a precondition for agreeing to the START treaty. This I consider to be patently unreasonable.

Purely arguing as a technician, one can maintain that linkage between constraints on ballistic missile defense and the strictures of START is not required. One can argue—and, for instance, Academician Sakharov has done so on earlier occasions—that the promise of SDI activities beyond the strictures of the ABM Treaty is so limited and the reductions proposed for START so moderate that for the next decade any feasible ABM deployment would make little difference strategically.

While I tend to agree with this conclusion, I would maintain that the sanctity of a treaty like the ABM Treaty, which has been agreed to by its signatories to be valid for an unlimited period, should be an overriding issue, unless there is a truly supreme national security interest.

Even within the traditional interpretation, there are many gray areas of conduct that could give rise to friction and mistrust in the future, unless the already established consultative mechanisms which provide a forum to clarify areas where one side questions the conduct of the other are used more effectively. Groups of technically competent delegates from the two sides should arrive at guidelines for accepted and forbidden conduct under the ABM Treaty.

In the spirit of glasnost, space activities coming close to the boundaries defined by the ABM Treaty should be disclosed to a consultative body, in which the legality of proposed missions can be discussed. While such a body cannot veto activities in the gray area of conduct, discussions of the purported space missions can go a long way to preventing future disputes.

While START will be an extraordinarily important agreement, no one can justly claim that START will substantially, let alone drastically, change the relationship between the superpowers in itself. The enactment of START will in no way require a revision of the strategic doctrine now established by either government, although the target lists will have to be moderately shortened.

But one should legitimately ask: How deep can reductions in strategic armaments of the superpowers be before the basic relationship between the superpowers and the doctrinal base of acquiring and deploying strategic nuclear weapons must be altered? This is an important question.

A partial answer is provided by a recent study carried out at the incentive of our committee. This study makes it clear that under reductions by a factor of two these relationships will hardly change at all, and that, in fact, this conclusion is rather insensitive to the detailed mixture of forces remaining after the reductions are accomplished. Even reductions by a factor of four need not change the relationships, although some care in how to achieve such reductions should be exercised for this conclusion to remain valid.

Thus, the more moderate reductions contemplated for START will have little impact, other than in the purely political and symbolic sense. Financial savings may or may not accrue, depending on separate unilateral decisions on modernization of the strategic forces.

But this remark does in no way make START less important. START will materially expedite the many adjustments that are evolving between the superpowers, and it can save money and reduce the demand for resources, in particular those for nuclear materials.

The unequivocal conclusion of these studies is that there is no technical need for linkage between pushing for speedy completion of START and other negotiations that are aimed at alleviating some of the problems which beset the relationship between the superpowers, particularly those relating to Western Europe. In other words, one cannot argue that one should go slow at START until other negotiations have run their course.

In view of the above, the remaining obstacles to START should be resolvable in the first, or at most the second, year of the Bush Administration. While it is understandable that the new national security team of the Bush Administration wishes to review these issues on its own, there are those who are promoting a deliberate go-slow attitude. The reasons expressed for caution generally fall under some combination of four arguments: (1) the credibility of the nuclear deterrent for the defense of Europe should not be further undermined, beyond what the INF Treaty has already done; (2) the current categorization of different reductions proposed at START does not maximize stability and does not eliminate the perceived vulnerability of the land-based ICBM force in the United States; (3) SDI flexibility should not be limited in any way, notwithstanding the ABM Treaty or the limited technical or budgetary expectations for SDI; or (4) verification measures for START are either inadequate, too expensive, or both. Let me separately address these four possible objections to going forward speedily now with START.

Currently, the United States' protection of Western Europe rests on the doctrine of what is known as extended deterrence. This doctrine is based on the presumption that the Warsaw Pact nations are superior in conventional arms over NATO and that the extent of that superiority is sufficient to permit a sudden attack by the Warsaw Pact against NATO by concentrating forces on selected points on the European frontier.

It is argued that the credibility of having the nuclear forces controlled by the United States come to the aid of Europe in case of a threatened defeat of NATO forces would be undermined by START. Critics claim that the impact of the INF Treaty and the rhetoric on the total elimination of nuclear weapons at Reykjavik have already diminished European faith in the United States' nuclear commitment.

The basic question of redressing the conventional balance will be the task of the forthcoming Conventional Forces in Europe (CFE) talks and has already been addressed in part by Gorbachev's unilateral move to withdraw 50,000 Soviet troops from the territory of the Warsaw Pact allies and to reduce military forces by 500,000 worldwide. Moreover, Shevardnadze has promised that the Soviet Union will remove additional nuclear weapons from Europe.

However, even the most optimistic arms controllers would agree that, due to its fundamental complexity, an acceptable settlement of the European military balance from its current risk of sudden attack to a purely defensive posture will take several years to achieve. Paul Doty will address this matter later in this seminar. Thus, making a settlement of the European balance a precondition to START would doom this next step in strategic nuclear force reduction for a long time.

There is no technical or military necessity for holding rapid action on nuclear strategic force reductions hostage to a settlement of the conventional balance in Europe. The types of calculations such as the ones referred to above make it clear that the proposed START reductions should not affect a presidential decision on whether or not to come to the aid of Europe in case of threatened conventional defeat.

However, the problem remains that the credibility as to whether a president would or would not make such a fateful decision is not based on technical or military factors alone, and therefore this argument will not subside under technical analysis. An irrational fear that any decrease in nuclear weapons within the homelands of the United States and the Soviet Union or on European soil would signal a decreased commitment to extended deterrence applied to Europe should not be permitted to detract from the urgency of lowering the total worldwide nuclear deployments from the insanely high levels we have today. In fact, almost all European leaders have urged the early enactment of a START treaty.

There can be, and always will be, debate about the optimal mixture of systems to be reduced by each side under an agreement such as START. Negotiable formulas will always be asymmetrical, because the point of departure from which the reductions are to be achieved and the geographical conditions are not symmetrical.

The START proposal on the table in Geneva has many laudable features—for instance, the special provision that reduces the large heavy missiles of the Soviet Union by half. However, as critics are prone to point out, neither START nor the now-lapsed SALT Treaty remedies the vulnerability of U.S. land-based ICBMs to presumed preemptive Soviet attack, nor were START or SALT ever designed to do that.

However, as many analyses, including that of the Scowcroft Commission on Strategic Forces, have conclusively pointed out, this vulnerability of the land-based forces cannot be exploited by the Soviet Union, since neither the U.S. nor the Soviet deterrent rests on the capability of the land-based forces alone. In fact, only roughly a quarter of U.S. strategic warheads are carried by its land-based ICBMs. These analyses have pointed out that the timing sequence that is involved in any preemptive attack against the strategic forces would make it impossible to attack the U.S. land-based forces without the attack against either element of strategic forces giving advance warning. In other words, the different legs of the strategic retaliatory forces are mutually reinforcing, so that an isolated attack against one of them is not a possibility. The so-called window of vulnerability is therefore a fiction.

A certain prescription for sabotaging the prospects of any strategic arms reduction agreement in the near future is to demand that it remedy the vulnerability of the land-based ICBM forces. This cannot be done by mutual agreement alone, but only in conjunction with redesigning the basing of such forces in such a way that a successful attack on these forces would exhaust a substantial fraction of the forces available to the attacker.

The next argument against proceeding now with START is promoted by SDI enthusiasts, who, notwithstanding the pessimistic prognostication for the ballistic missile defense systems deployable in the near future, insist that the United States should shed its obligations under the ABM Treaty. Such voices are, however, decreasing in numbers, when faced by the realities of technology and cost.

Then there is the problem of verification. The INF Treaty has broken new ground in reaching agreement between the United States and the Soviet Union, initiating highly intrusive verification measures by which compliance with the INF Treaty can be policed. We will hear details of the initial success of implementing the INF agreement in this respect from General Lajoie. Clearly, the START agreement will build on this important precedent.

While disagreements remain, most analysts would agree that verification provisions now on the table in Geneva are "adequate" in that they would reveal violations that have significant military importance. If violations were discovered, lead time would be available sufficient to respond effectively to such violations.

However, it is generally agreed that a START treaty will be more complex to verify than the zero-zero solution of the INF Treaty. It is clearly less difficult to verify elimination of a whole class of weapons, as the INF Treaty does, than to count and measure the numbers and performance of permitted strategic delivery systems under constraints negotiated under START.

Much has been made of the verification issue in the past, and such debates will continue. Actually, the record of compliance of nations with past arms control agreements has been excellent. Interestingly enough, the record is persuasive that even those treaties such as SALT I, SALT II, the Threshold Test Ban Treaty (limiting the size of nuclear test explosions), and the ABM Treaty have all, in fact, been obeyed throughout by all parties, with only minor exceptions which have no significant military importance. This is particularly noteworthy since among those treaties just cited only the ABM Treaty is actually in force, while the other treaties have been signed but not ratified. SALT I has lapsed in time, and SALT II has been officially abrogated by the U.S. Administration. Thus, signed treaties have in fact been a very powerful force in limiting the conduct of nations, and each party has elected in its own enlightened self-interest to comply in all essential respects. Such treaties have limited the more extreme "worst case projections" that intelligence analysts can introduce.

Thus, I would conclude, although the matter of verification and promoting compliance is a highly important matter, that those who object to the enactment of proposed treaties on grounds of inadequate verification measures are, in fact, generally objecting to the provisions of the treaty itself, using alleged inadequacy of verification as a cover.

To summarize, with mutual goodwill between the Bush Administration and the Soviets, a clear path exists to negotiating the remaining obstacles to START, and I see no validity to any of the go-slow arguments counseling against speedy conclusion of that treaty.

It is clear that START is not the end of the road as far as desirable strategic arms reductions are concerned. Further reductions by at least another factor of two could be pursued bilaterally with the Soviet Union. Further reductions beyond that would require involvement with the other nuclear nations, in particular China, France, and Great Britain. Thus, concurrent with completing START and completing one further step in the reduction of strategic arms, arms control should focus on other agenda, most of which can only be negotiated in a multilateral, rather than a bilateral, forum.

Enactment of START can and should proceed rapidly. However, the above discussion makes it clear that truly major reductions of strategic nuclear weapons could not be accomplished unless and until the United States would find it possible to modify its current doctrine of extended deterrence. Under that doctrine, U.S. strategic nuclear weapons are to deter not only aggression with nuclear weapons but also the initiation of conventional attack, in particular in Western Europe. If extended deterrence is interpreted under current doctrine, this requires that a surviving retaliatory force should be able to destroy the war-making potential of the aggressor.

Although there is increasing doubt concerning the credibility of the United States' nuclear umbrella, it is clear that a conservative interpretation of U.S. national security interests would not permit shifting from the current extended deterrence doctrine until threats to European security from Soviet attack by conventional forces are no longer considered feasible.

Although I agree that, particularly with the recent shift in Soviet attitudes, the possibility of such aggression is indeed extremely remote, it remains a technical possibility unless the perceived inferiority of NATO in conventional arms is redressed. Thus, the ongoing and forthcoming negotiations aimed at enhancing stability in Europe are of overriding importance.

The multinational negotiations designed to limit the spread of chemical weapons will hopefully soon be brought to successful conclusion. The threat of chemical warfare has recently become a great public concern as a result of the use of such weapons by Iraq. These talks in the 40-nation Conference on Disarmament go beyond the Geneva Convention prohibition against use of chemical weapons in their aim to prohibit manufacture and stockpiling as well. These talks have made enormous progress. In fact, the Soviets and the United States have provisionally accepted inspection provisions that would have been unimaginable a few years ago.

The principal threat here is not the use of chemical weapons in a U.S.-Soviet conflict but the increasing worldwide proliferation of such weapons. Professor Meselson will discuss this matter in detail later.

Similarly, a new focus has been placed on clarifying the situation in regard to biological weapons. Here the existing Biological Weapons Convention prohibits the manufacture of such weapons but permits defensive measures and unlimited research. There are no commonly accepted verification provisions, and the quantities of biological agents that can be justified for conducting research or to exercise defensive measures are not restricted.

While the technology of chemical weapons has not advanced substantially since World War II, biotechnology of possible relevance to biological warfare is a very dynamic field, and therefore there is an urgent need to tighten restrictions in that area. A subcommittee of our group has been active in this matter.

The issue of nonproliferation of nuclear weapons will again be in critical focus due to the impending review conference in 1990 and the definitive review conference in 1995. The threat of the threshold countries joining the nuclear club is very real. Moreover, nuclear weapons raw materials have themselves become threats to the environment, indicating that the real cost of such materials is much higher than has been presumed. These issues must be faced now. Mr. Keeny will discuss this later.

The afternoon session of this seminar will be devoted to those forthcoming arms control moves, other than those dedicated to the central problem of controlling strategic arms, which I have outlined. In turn, should those additional arms control moves prove fruitful, then modifying current strategic doctrine to reduce the role of strategic nuclear weapons solely to deter a nuclear attack, not nuclear *and* conventional attacks, should become feasible. In turn, this reduced role requires a much smaller number of nuclear weapons.

Thus, while total elimination of nuclear weapons does not appear to be a feasible goal in the present international order, we can look forward in the future to a world with hundreds rather than tens of thousands of nuclear weapons.

3

Soviet "New Thinking" About International Security

Roald Sagdeev

When important changes take place in international life—especially in the area of military confrontation—they are generally signified by treaties. However, one very important event will probably never be confirmed by the signing of a treaty: I am speaking now about the end of the Cold War.[1]

I have a proposal to offer as testimony that the Cold War is over. This proposal is to rename Sakharov Plaza the "Plaza of People's Deputy Sakharov."

There is a general consensus that the Cold War, even if it is over now, has left us with a tremendous overabundance of weapons—a tremendous "overarming." A couple of decades ago we introduced the term "overkill" while speaking about strategic nuclear weapons. But with an increasing recognition of the importance of a coherent approach, an integral approach, we are now speaking more and more about an overabundance of conventional weapons. So there is a conceptual understanding, perhaps a kind of consensus, that the very existence of overarming itself is very dangerous.

Yet at the same time, there is no factual development that would bring us hope that we are moving toward a world without overarming. All that is going on now are individual talks and negotiations, with no integral approach toward solving the problem of overarming. There are fundamental differences in every individual negotiation. Only with a coherent global approach to reduce overarming can we achieve real success.

The "new thinking" promoted by General Secretary Mikhail Gorbachev during his first four years in power is now evolving toward the formulation of such a global system of common, or mutual, security—a system that would provide a chance for the coherent development of future military configurations based on a drastic reduction of overarming.

The reasons for this enormous overarming are quite obvious: the Cold War and many other unfortunate parallel developments. One of the important elements on our side is that we are now ready to recognize, to confess, that on many occasions and in many instances, the Soviet side was not clever enough. We were often ready to follow the Western lead in developing new military technologies and new armaments. However, we did not resist enough, as we say now, being provoked to participate in the arms race. We did not recognize the importance that political steps, political methods, could have had in strengthening international security. Indeed, in some cases we ourselves were the driving force for the "hard line." The present Soviet government recognizes that we made a number of errors and mistakes in military doctrine and in the actual development of our military system.

On the basis of such confessions and recognition, the Soviet government has taken unilateral steps in many areas. I am talking about a rather long list of different unilateral moratoriums, not all of them successful. Let me remind you that the first unilateral step was a moratorium on antisatellite weapons (ASATs), declared in August 1983. I consider this moratorium to have been a very successful step, especially since it was reciprocated by the American Congress. In fact, after six years, both sides still have this kind of de facto bilateral moratorium on ASAT testing and development.

Another important unilateral step taken by our side was a reduction of conventional armaments both in Europe and Asia. This particular step was based on a recognition that there is a linkage between strategic and conventional forces, and a political linkage between negotiations on strategic nuclear arms control and conventional arms control, in Europe especially.

I fully agree with Professor Panofsky that these linkages should never be formalized to such an extent as to stop progress on any individual element of arms control.

I would like to complement the figures that he gave on strategic forces with some figures on conventional armaments, and show you the official figures that are given by the Soviet side and by the Warsaw Treaty Organization.

Table I[1] summarizes the most recent interview given by Defense Minister General Dimitri Yazov, only two days ago. These figures deal with many kinds of armaments. They are integral figures, reflecting what is actually in the arsenals of the Warsaw Treaty Organization and NATO. They do not include nuclear warheads or special strategic delivery systems, except military aircraft. Manpower is counted in millions. In the figures given by General Yazov, there is a noticeable asymmetry in favor of NATO. I am not going to discuss whether these figures are consistent with Western presentations.

General Yazov argues that there is no integral military imbalance between the Warsaw Treaty Organization and NATO. He bases his argument on figures given in response to some of the statements made by the new Secretary of Defense, Mr. Cheney. These numbers include military aircraft (excluding cargo planes), tanks, and surface ships. Some of the numbers for surface ships are rather conditional. For example, not every kind of ship is counted, only ships above a certain size—something like 1,200 tons, I think. Then there are aircraft carriers and surface ships equipped with different kinds of cruise missiles. These are overall world-wide numbers. Later on I will give you the Warsaw Treaty interpretation for conventional figures in Europe.

Together with the figures given by Professor Panofsky on nuclear forces, I think this provides a complete integral picture of the existing balance. There is a strong imbalance in the number of tanks. One of the most important arguments on the Soviet side is that this substantial advantage for the Warsaw Treaty Organization is compensated for by two factors: part by NATO's advantage in strike aircraft and strike helicopters, and, in major part, by a strong NATO advantage in naval forces, including naval forces currently deployed in and near Europe.

On the basis of such obvious disparities, the Soviet Union declared its intention to carry out some unilateral reductions. I will not give you the detailed figures, but personnel will be decreased on the Soviet side by a bit more than 500,000. The number of tanks will be decreased by 10,000, a fewer number of artillery guns, and a small number of aircraft. General Yazov confirmed in his last interview that at present, on April 21, 1989—so the figure is very fresh (it still would be the same two days later)—700 tanks were withdrawn from Eastern Europe, from East Germany, Czechoslovakia, and Poland, along with a number of troops. So the process of unilateral reduction to decrease disparities is already in action.

Reductions will also be seen in the figures of our military budget. I cannot argue about the size of our military budget; the figures are not yet published. While running to become a People's Deputy, I promised to my electorate that I would insist on the publication of such figures. Some relative figures have been given by the government, however. The reduction in military spending for 1989 is 1.5 percent, including all kinds of military expenditures—decreased production by the military industry, and so on. In 1990, military expenditures will decrease 7 percent, and in 1991, a decrease of up to 14.2 percent is promised.

By that time, I am sure we will know not only the relative figures, but also the absolute figures. I hope they will be published within the next three or four months, maybe even earlier.[2]

Table II indicates corresponding figures related to European conventional forces. I took them from the long document issued by the Warsaw Treaty Organization in January 1989 in response to an identical NATO document published in late November 1988. These figures indicate that there is a balance in manpower, and a rather reasonable balance in the number of combat aircraft, counted as the sum of tactical, naval, and air defense. There is a substantial advantage on the side of the Warsaw Treaty Organization in interceptor aircraft, but these interceptors are considered by the Warsaw Treaty Organization to be unable to attack ground-based targets—they can only act against objects in the air. Yet this imbalance is compensated for, roughly, by an advantage in naval aircraft and strike aircraft on the side of NATO.

There is also a considerable disparity in the number of combat helicopters in NATO's favor, but a substantial advantage on the side of the Warsaw Treaty Organization in tanks. So out of 80,000 tanks, almost 60,000 are attributed to the European theater. To some extent, this is compensated for by NATO's approximately 1.6 to 1 advantage in antitank rockets and rocket-launching complexes.

Again, looking at integral figures for naval forces, the numbers for the European theater are in favor of NATO, especially in aircraft carriers.

Several key military figures on the Soviet side[3] recently suggested that the process of eliminating disparities in force balances in Europe should be extended to naval forces. Otherwise, there will be a substantial NATO advantage in naval forces. This is all I will say about the existing figures.

The concept we are developing now of how to proceed on our side is to make a very important development in the conventional arms area. We should keep in mind that it would be extremely difficult to achieve a completely symmetrical situation. Professor Panofsky was speaking about the origin of asymmetries, the origin of asymmetries coming from geographical, geopolitical, and historical reasons. It would be naive to hope to eliminate all these asymmetries at once.

It is quite clear that such a great disparity in land-based forces derives from our history, especially during the last years of World War II and the postwar period. I do not think we could ever base our military doctrine on reestablishing parity in the oceans and in the seas. This gives our military an additional argument as to why we should keep ourselves a little bit stronger on land.

Even if we reach a common language, a common understanding, about the overall balance and the inevitability of disparities, there is the even more complicated issue of stability. We have spent many years trying to reach a common definition of nuclear stability. I think we are now very close to having a consensus about the criteria for strategic stability. Still, conventional stability is a new area, and we are only now entering this new land. The conventional forces reduction talks now under way in Europe should contribute a lot to the development of a common formula for, and a common definition of, conventional stability.

Working from these two important conceptual understandings—strategic nuclear stability and conventional stability—we can try to develop a joint approach to coherent arms reduction in both spheres. However, it may take rather a long time to come to such a consensus.

I agree with Professor Panofsky that, even with existing disagreements on strategic and conventional stability, we should not delay the START talks or talks on conventional arms reductions in Europe until we reach such a consensus in the conceptual area.

It is very important that we extend the definition of stability to actions on the seas and the oceans. In that case, the definition of stability would also include important geographical restrictions or agreements, the creation of special ocean zones, and mutual confidence-building measures. This is a completely open area right now.

Negotiations and discussions that have nothing to do with nuclear or conventional stability are now going on in parallel at different levels. These talks concern chemical and biological weapons. We consider it very important to have parallel success in these areas, because success in these areas, where we have almost no disagreements in concept, will strengthen our positions in nuclear and conventional negotiations.

We are approaching the time when strategic nuclear stability may enter into conflict with the process of the gradual—it may be slow, but still it is moving—approach of several nations to the nuclear threshold. If we ourselves are unable to make important progress in strategic nuclear arms control, it will be even more difficult to prevent an increased number of nations from approaching the nuclear threshold. The situation will become especially dangerous if both sides are unable to agree on nonmodernization of nuclear weapons. Nonmodernization can be achieved by nuclear test bans. The time has come once again to reconsider our mutual stance on nuclear testing.

We are making important progress now in cutting off the production of fissile materials. The Soviet government has decided to introduce measures to eliminate plutonium production and to shut down several plants that produce enriched uranium. In fact, these plants are environmentally and technologically obsolete. Our understanding is that the United States also has old-fashioned, obsolete plants. This, therefore, is a very convenient moment to mutually agree on some parallel steps.

We are rapidly approaching 1995, when the Treaty on Nuclear Non-Proliferation will have to be reaffirmed or extended. This is an important problem, again related to the issue of limiting the number of nuclear nations and the number of subnuclear nations approaching the threshold.

If these rather modest parallel talks are successful, then the next step on our side will be discussions about the introduction of the concept of "reasonable sufficiency." This concept was suggested by Gorbachev two years ago and was supported conceptually by the Warsaw Treaty Organization, but only as a concept. There is no concrete military doctrine developed as an interpretation of reasonable sufficiency. Some experts say that unilateral steps now under way are in the spirit of this reasonable sufficiency concept, but most experts think that reasonable sufficiency cannot be developed unilaterally—it should be a mutual, global step.

There are a few preliminary ideas about how to define reasonable sufficiency. In the area of strategic nuclear weapons, there is a tentative desire to compare reasonable sufficiency with the older concept of minimum deterrence. I agree with Professor Panofsky, who essentially, without using such terminology, was speaking about hundreds of nuclear warheads on each side as a desirable threshold, compared with the tens of thousands existing now.

Nuclear or strategic reasonable sufficiency probably will not be established without the participation of the other nuclear nations. This is the post-START stage, which, from the very beginning, was envisaged as being multinational.

There is a strong temptation to develop the concept of reasonable sufficiency in the area of conventional forces on the basis of an intrinsic tie with the concept of "defensive defense." There are many interesting ideas about how this defensive defense could be configured.

A similar idea could be extended to naval forces. There is a lot of discussion on the defensive defense posture for land-based forces, but very little discussion for naval forces. So a first idea would be, for example, to start with those components of naval forces that could be considered offensive—such as aircraft carriers, ships that can deliver weapons, and so on. With such restructuring, naval forces could be given more and more defensive features.

Another important issue concerns how to deal with subnuclear nations—the nations that are gradually approaching the nuclear threshold. Only combined global actions will be sufficient. Some actions in the area of the economy and international trade would involve establishing special types of embargoes, and, very importantly, cutting military trade.

There is a very important issue of regional conflicts. This area was recently accorded very great importance, and we already are seeing several tentative successes in regulating regional conflicts.

It would also be important to include in the concept of reasonable sufficiency the ability of the responsible nations to counteract or to fight against terrorism, whether it be individual, nongovernmental, or governmental terrorism, religious fanaticism, or other things of this kind.

All these measures would require the actual perestroika of international relations, which would touch not only military issues, but also economic and political issues. It is very difficult to separate the issues of international perestroika and international life from the perestroika that is going on inside my own country. I have already mentioned some unilateral steps. There are also other very important changes occurring in my country, both in its economy and, probably most important, in its political life.

Many candidates for People's Deputies—some of them have already been elected—had in their programs important statements on military doctrine and arms control. One of the most important elements of my program, literally included in the published version, was to establish the people's control over the Soviet military-industrial complex. Some of the Deputies went into more detail and called for the establishment of control over the KGB.[4]

It is very difficult to change perceptions. One of the most difficult problems we now face is that we have to deal with perceptions. For example, I recently discovered that one of the groups in your country conducted a special public opinion poll that asked, "What would constitute the most dangerous threat to the life of Americans?" To my complete surprise, I discovered that the Soviet nuclear threat—a military threat— won only 13th place. It is nice that the image of us as the enemy is fading, but at the same time it was a shock, and somehow also a great humiliation for the Russians. Here we have sacrificed to create this superstrong military machine, overarming. We sacrificed many aspects of our material life. The most recent sacrifice being that last week, even in Moscow, sugar was rationed—I hope this is not an outcome of the recent meeting between Gorbachev and Castro.

I think we should always consider what is going on in the area of people's perceptions. On our side there has also been an important change: a decreased perception of the American military threat. For example, almost no candidate for People's Deputy put forward slogans calling for us to support a military buildup to counter the American threat.

---

[1]Editor's note: The two tables referred to in this talk were unavailable for publication.

[2]In June 1989, at the Congress of People's Deputies, the overall military budget was given as 77 billion rubles.

[3]In July 1989, Marshal Sergei Akhromeyev reiterated this while visiting the United States.

[4]The Supreme Soviet in July 1989 established the Committee on Defense and the KGB.

4

The INF Treaty: A Status Report on INF Inspections

Roland Lajoie

Last August I led a group of American inspectors into the Soviet Union to witness the first elimination of a Soviet missile to be destroyed under the INF Treaty. The inspection took place at Kapustin Yar, a missile test facility that is about three hours east of Volgograd. During the preliminary inspection my On-Site Inspection Agency (OSIA) inspectors were allowed complete access to the missiles, which were in their canister. Both ends of the canister had been opened, allowing the inspectors to perform the requisite measurements and reassure themselves that this, in fact, was an SS-20 that was being eliminated. A sudden rainstorm interrupted this process and several inspectors moved inside the missile canister to get out of the rain.

I thought to myself that four years ago as an Army attaché in Moscow had I been within 100 miles of that facility, I would have found myself in a very, very difficult situation. And yet here we were a group of American inspectors not only on a secret missile test facility, but blithely stepping inside a missile canister to get out of the rain as though it were the most natural thing to do. To my mind this one incident more clearly than anything else illustrates the dizzying changes that are occurring in U.S.-Soviet relationships.

What I would like to tell you about today, then, is the "Road to Kapustin Yar." In other words to explain to you, in very nonabstract terms, what the U.S. Government is doing to implement the INF Treaty. I have a series of slides that will help me tell this story. I think you will find it interesting.

The road to Kapustin Yar began last December in Washington when President Reagan and General Secretary Gorbachev signed the INF Treaty. Six months later, on 1 June 1988, the instruments of ratification were exchanged at the Moscow summit. Exactly 30 days later both sides began inspecting each other's INF bases.

The INF Treaty is in fact not a single document but rather a basic treaty, two additional protocols to tell me in considerable detail how to conduct my inspections and what qualifies as an elimination and, finally, a memorandum of understanding (MOU) that lists all the INF systems covered by the treaty, their numbers, characteristics, and locations.

I will just remind you at this point that the INF Treaty is not in any fashion "an anyplace, anytime" inspection regime. I can only conduct inspections of those 133 inspectable activities listed in the MOU and must limit my inspections to those specific systems covered by the treaty.

During the initial round of baseline inspections while verifying the technical data in the MOU, we were able to do some very, very detailed kinds of measurements that required intrusive access to the systems, on an unprecedented scale. Take for instance the SS-20. The Soviets indicated initially that this missile becomes so unstable outside its environmentally controlled canister that it is never removed from its canister, and therefore we could not have access to it. And eventually we were permitted access. The missile was taken out of its canister, broken down into its two stages, and then those stages were measured and weighed by our inspectors, using in all cases American devices. This was to my mind an impressively intrusive procedure.

I would like now to discuss OSIA's mission and will attempt to limit myself exclusively to my specific responsibilities that have to do with inspections; I did not negotiate the treaty; I have no responsibilities for the policy implications of the treaty. I do inspections, record my findings, and send the data back to Washington, where the broader compliance judgments are made.

Below are the five kinds of inspections my agency does:

Baseline Inspections. This process to verify the declared inventory in the MOU was conducted in the first two months after Entry into Force of the Treaty (July–August 1988). This meant that we were required in 60 days to travel throughout the Soviet Union, visit each of those 133 facilities that had an INF mission, and verify all of the data contained in the MOU.

Elimination Inspections. Each accountable item that is eliminated under the treaty is done so in the presence of our inspectors and according to the detailed procedures spelled out in the elimination protocol. When we are completely satisfied that the elimination processes have been carried out exactly as they should be, we sign the inspection report.

Close-out Inspections. After an INF missile base or other related installation has had its INF systems removed to the designated elimination facility and any INF-unique infrastructure has been eliminated, that base gets inspected. Our inspectors arrive, confirm that the base can no longer support an INF role, and sign an inspection report to that effect. You understand that many of those INF bases can and will be converted to another military use. An SS-20 base for instance could actually be turned into an SS-25 base; the Soviets are merely required to notify us of this conversion. We of course will have the right to utilize a quota inspection to gain access to the converted facility during the 13-year life of the treaty. We would at that point be checking to ensure that whatever new military function has been introduced to this base is *not* an INF system. Even for a former INF facility—for instance, the one in Czechoslovakia—that has been totally closed out and reportedly will be converted to a sanatorium, we can, if we choose, revisit it at any point during the life of the treaty.

Short-Notice Inspections. These are the decreasing quota inspections that we will be conducting for the 13-year life of the treaty. For whatever reason we can decide on a short-notice basis to check and recheck any INF installation covered by the treaty.

Portal Monitoring. Finally, the most unique aspect of the entire treaty is what is called portal perimeter monitoring. This is where each side permanently stations a group of inspectors at a missile production or assembly facility that formerly produced INF systems. These portal monitors will stay there for the life of the treaty (on a rotational basis of course!), monitoring any production leaving the plant to make sure that it includes no prohibited system.

The American side, particularly, insisted on this aspect during treaty negotiations. The U.S. portal is located at a Soviet missile assembly plant in the Urals, near a small city called Votkinsk. Votkinsk formerly produced the SS-20 missiles and currently produces the SS-25. The SS-25, as you know, is a mobile ICBM, whose external configurations are quite similar to those of the SS-20. This meant that the United States wanted to be able to closely monitor this activity and make sure that only SS-25's and not SS-20's were leaving the plant to constitute some kind of a covert IRBM force.

The baseline inventory had to be completed in 60 days. This meant taking this brand-new organization that had never done inspections and immediately plunging into the most hectic period of our responsibilities, averaging two inspections every single day during July and August of 1988.

That is all behind us. Now we will be conducting a decreasing number of quota inspections, monitor the portal at Votkinsk (where we will have Americans for the next 13 years), watch eliminations, and check closed-out bases.

So three years from now (unless we pick up additional responsibilities in the conventional or START arenas), OSIA will have a very modest mission—the portal, which by then would hopefully become a rather sleepy night watchman's activity, and decreasing quota inspections.

Just to remind you, the systems that are covered by the treaty on the Soviet side are:

1. the SSC-X-4, a developed, but nondeployed, cruise missile;
2. the shorter-range SS-12 and SS-23;
3. the older SS-4's and SS-5's; and, finally,
4. the intermediate-range SS-20, which particularly concerned us.

These systems are scattered across 117 different locations throughout the Soviet Union, East Germany, and Czechoslovakia.

On the U.S. side, the systems covered by the treaty and subject to Soviet inspections are the (1) ground-launched cruise missile (GLCM), (2) the Pershing II, and (3) the shorter-range and older Pershing IA.

Those systems are located in the United States and at our basing countries in Western Europe—some 32 separate inspectable sites to which the Soviet inspectors have access.

As you can see, I have a very considerable inspection responsibility covering those 133 inspectable activities at 117 separate locations while my escort responsibilities are somewhat modest, because there are not that many Soviet inspectors coming over. My counterpart, General Medvedev, has to devote much more attention to his escort apparatus because he has Americans in his area at all times. Today, I have 87 Americans in the Soviet Union conducting inspections, while 41 of General Medvedev's people are being hosted at U.S. bases.

My mission is relatively straightforward: organize everything that is necessary to place the right group of American inspectors at the right place at the right time and then coordinate all activities associated with making sure that the Soviet inspectors are provided the opportunity to discharge their treaty responsibilities at our sites. I like this feature of having both sides of the coin. I do the inspections, and I facilitate and control the Soviet inspectors. Reciprocity playing such a large role in this treaty, it is useful to be involved in and directly influence both aspects.

Let me say something about the concept of operation that we developed when we were presented with the INF Treaty for implementation. I will not go into any details about how we created this organization from the ground up. We were handed the treaty and told to set up an organization that was capable of discharging the U.S. Government's responsibilities. Suffice it to say that it was a very, very exciting prospect of starting with a blank sheet of paper and building the basic organization, a supporting infrastructure, and the concept of operation—exciting but at the same time daunting.

Given the geographical spread of our inspection responsibilities and very tight time lines dictated by the treaty, it became clear that we would not be able to support the number of inspections required of us. Attempting to launch all our inspections from the United States would have risked missing our time windows. After coordinating with the governments of Japan and Germany we decided to establish "gateways" at Yakota Air Force Base in Japan and at Rhein Main Air Force Base in Germany. We then forward deployed our forces there and set up a briefing/debriefing apparatus and small operations/logistics cell to support the inspections. This allowed our inspectors to cycle into the Soviet Union and back to those gateways and back into the USSR without returning all the way to the United States.

To support this concept and meet all of the escort missions necessitated the creation of an infrastructure that spreads across 19 time zones. As you can see on the map, we have a small element in San Francisco that is responsible for receiving Soviet inspectors arriving in the United States to conduct inspections in the western part of the United States or rotating in or out of the Soviet portal. Out in Magna, Utah, is the Hercules plant that used to produce the Pershing II rocket motors and where the Soviets have their portal perimeter monitoring facility. There are 30 Soviets located there, and I have a similar number of Americans escorting the Soviets and making sure that all goes well.

OSIA headquarters is located in Washington. In Frankfurt, Germany, as I mentioned, we have two activities: a reception center for all Soviet inspectors coming in to conduct inspections at our basing countries in Western Europe and the gateway to process our people enroute to the Soviet Union from Washington.

In Moscow, because Ambassador Jack Matlock said that there was no way under his current diplomatic personnel ceilings that he could support this level of inspection activity in the USSR, we negotiated very quickly with the Soviets to raise the ceilings so that a six-person diplomatic aircrew escort contingent could be added to the embassy staff.

The U.S. portal facility is located at the Votkinsk missile assembly plant in the Urals. And over here, east of Lake Baikal, is the eastern point of entry, Ulan Ude, through which we access the 33 inspectable sites in Siberia and the Far East. There are two Americans at this distant INF outpost to meet, greet, and facilitate OSIA inspectors. One is a Foreign Service officer, and her husband happens to be a Navy SEABEE noncommissioned officer assigned to OSIA. It is an interesting little interagency team. And, finally, over here in Japan, as I mentioned, we have a small cell to take care of our inspectors transitioning Yokota enroute to the USSR.

Inspection Teams. Forming inspection teams is not really a complicated matter. The treaty says that we can have 200 approved inspectors on a list and no more than 10 inspectors on one site (except for eliminations when the limit is 20) at any particular time. Early on we just divided all our resources into twenty 10-man teams. We provided each with a sprinkling of the kinds of talents that you would want on your side if you were going on to a Soviet installation to inspect missile activity. We also try to tailor the teams for each facility. Going on to an SS-20 missile-operating base, for instance, we would have more SS-20 specialists than if we went to an SS-4 storage facility. The team chief is currently a military officer, usually a lieutenant colonel, or navy commander. The deputy team chief is invariably a USG civilian who probably has some Soviet-area expertise. We also have missile-operating specialists who are those young military officers and noncommissioned officers coming out of the Pershing or GLCM units that are being disbanded. We include them into the team to provide us with a "blue" perspective. We find that they make a unique contribution. Then there are two dedicated military linguists and finally the technical specialists and the analysts. The latter come from the various government agencies and provide us with the technical know-how, so that when we arrive at a site we know exactly what we are looking at.

The most important person on that team is not the specialist who has been studying SS-20's for a dozen years or the analyst or the linguist, but rather the team leader. Leading that disparate collection of specialists into the Soviet Union requires a good, strong leader. He is the key individual. We want to make sure that these people know what they are doing, that the U.S. Government discharges its treaty responsibilities.

Escort Teams. Soviet INF inspectors in the United States or Western Europe are not diplomats, and they are certainly not tourists. They are inspectors with privileges and immunities that are somewhat less than those of a diplomat or military attaché. That means that their baggage is subject to search, and they themselves are constantly escorted during their inspections. Once again for escort purposes there is an obvious distribution of specialties required to adequately perform this function. And here again the OSIA team chief is carefully picked. It is he who is the official interpreter of the treaty for the U.S. Government.

As you might imagine, coordinating all this activity at each of our INF bases in the United States and with all of the basing countries in Europe was a complicated challenge that we faced early last spring. The Dutch and the Belgians and the Germans and the British and the Italians each have a slightly different interpretation of what "full escort" means. Since the INF Treaty is a bilateral accord, we had to ensure that there was a coherent and consistent U.S. Government approach while taking into account the understandable sovereignty concerns of our basing country allies.   Achieving a consistent but not necessarily identical approach required a lot of coordination. This prior coordination paid dividends, and actual implementation in Europe has been smooth indeed.

Soviet inspectors, as they arrive, are met by our escort personnel at plane side. As I say, inspectors are not diplomats. All of their luggage, to include any technical equipment, is subject to and routinely scrutinized by the Customs and Immigration people in Washington and San Francisco.

Within 30 hours or so of their arrival, we take the Soviet inspectors to the INF site they have designated, where they are allowed to do exactly what we do on an inspection, i.e., verify the numbers, locations, and technical characteristics of the systems that are covered by the treaty. In the course of visiting an installation the entire area specified in the treaty is visited and all buildings, sheds, or vehicles capable of storing a treaty-limited item are carefully inspected. Most of this is not complicated. These are large systems, and they have a very obvious physical signature. We do routinely measure the systems regardless of our familiarity with them. To exercise that right we also bring scales along during inspections to weigh items if we deem it necessary.

I will next quickly cover the portal monitoring sites to give you an idea of what happens there.

Votkinsk. Votkinsk is actually a missile assembly plant; it is not a production facility. Rocket motors, canisters, and other components are sent there from various factories for final assembly. As I mentioned, SS-20 missiles used to be assembled here and this accounts for the American presence, i.e., to make sure that all SS-20 activity has ceased. The problem is that SS-25's, which are three-stage mobile ICBMs, still come out of there, and we need to scrutinize these shipments to make sure that anything leaving is in fact an SS-25 and not an SS-20.

We have 30 Americans there. There are five OSIA officers who serve as overall supervisors of the facility and as the official interface with the plant officials and the Soviet escorts. The majority of the U.S. team is composed of civilian specialists from Hughes Technical Services Co., which bid on this project and won the contract.

I can tell you that we have what I would consider a very impressive array of technical monitoring equipment in Votkinsk to make sure that no SS-20's come out. There are of course TV cameras, seals, and in-ground sensors, so that any vehicle leaving the plant triggers an alarm inside our data collection center. We also have an infrared profiler that will automatically give you the external configuration of every item coming out of there and compare it against SS-20 statistics. We will shortly be shipping to the Soviet Union a rather large X-ray machine that additionally will give us the ability to look through every missile rail car leaving the plant.

Currently, missile rail cars coming out are stopped, measured, and entered. Inside we also examine and we measure the canister. Eight times a year we have the option of looking inside the canister. For such interior examinations the rail car is brought into a special building, where the front dome is removed, allowing our inspectors to look inside. Because it is difficult to see beyond the third stage, we are also negotiating with the Soviets on an optical-mechanical instrument that we will be able to insert inside the canister during such inspections to measure the second stage. It is the second stage that particularly concerns us, because it is within six inches of being identical to the second stage of an SS-20. We are thus poking around a Soviet ICBM to verify a treaty pertaining only to IRBM.

When we install the X-ray equipment, in addition to the above, we will routinely X-ray every single missile car that comes through the portal. This will allow us to look through the car, through the canister, and even through a portion of the missile, to make absolutely sure that there is not somehow a missile inside of a missile, as would be the case if Votkinsk were still assembling SS-20's and slipping them inside sleeves made to look like "legal" SS-25's. Such subterfuge at the one location in the Soviet Union where 30 Americans are permanently encamped may not be the most likely cheating scenario, but nonetheless it is one that the X-ray equipment will allow us to defeat.

Magna. Out at Magna, Utah, just outside Salt Lake City, is where the Hercules plant is located and where the Soviets exercised their reciprocal right to establish a perimeter monitoring facility. At Hercules the Pershing rocket motors were produced within a large complex that still produces other kinds of rocket motors. It was therefore necessary to isolate that portion of the complex involved in the Pershing production and enclose the area by double fence. At Magna there is a main portal where every item large enough to contain a Pershing has to come out through Soviet inspection and two other exits, also monitored by Soviet inspectors, where all other items too small to be Pershings come out.

Missile Eliminations. In the final analysis, what the INF treaty is all about is eliminating missiles. This, I can report to you, is moving along smoothly. There are various ways to count the numerous systems and components covered by the treaty. Missiles are easiest to remember: 1,846 Soviet missiles, 846 U.S. missiles. Please remember that for each missile there are many associated items such as canisters and launchers and various support structures. All total on the Soviet side, there are some 6,000 accountable items that have to be destroyed in front of U.S. inspectors.

I will show you how this happens. The U.S. side does eliminations at three locations in the United States and one in Germany. The Pershing launchers are cut up in accordance with the treaty in Germany, where they are currently deployed. Rather than shipping those launchers all the way back to the United States and using up C-5's and C-141's to do that, we cut them up at Hausen and sell the scrap there.

All the Pershing and GLCM missiles, however, are destroyed in the United States because we did not want to have that possible environmental concern given to our allies. The U.S. Army has decided that the safest and most efficient way to eliminate these rocket motors is to bolt them to a stand, set off the firing mechanism, and then burn off all of the solid-rocket fuel. Once the fuel has been expended, the rocket motor casing is crushed and the remnants buried on Army property. The two Pershing elimination sites are in Pueblo, Colorado, and Marshall, Texas; in both cases, as you know, warheads and guidance packages have been removed prior to elimination.

For ground-launched cruise missiles the process is even more straightforward. After fuel is drained, the missiles and canisters are simply sawed in half. The Air Force does this on a round-the-clock basis, usually over one weekend. Soviet inspectors are flown in, and the elimination process proceeds for 48 hours straight. Then the inspectors go home, and the Air Force gets ready for the next batch.

Given the asymmetrical nature of the INF Treaty, the Soviets end up with a lot more missile systems to destroy. Therefore, they have more sites dedicated to this process. They also elected to eliminate by launching, one of the methods that was available to each side. The United States decided not to exercise this option because of the costs and complexities involved. The Soviets, however, did launch 72 missiles (which a Soviet officer insisted to me was the "natural" death of a missile). Incidentally, every one of those 72 SS-20 missiles went off on time, as advertised, with none of the standby missiles needed.

The entire elimination process for each different missile system is spelled out in excruciating detail in the treaty. For instance, a preliminary inspection of each item to be destroyed is conducted. Inspectors examine and measure each item, certify that it is the right missile, move back to a safe point, and then the item is blown in their presence. Although the results even from a safe distance are clearly unambiguous, our inspectors are required to go back to the site and make sure that, in fact, there is absolutely nothing left.

We are currently about one-third of the way into the elimination period, and in fact both sides are slightly ahead of schedule. The Soviets, I believe, have eliminated about 46 percent of their missile inventory and we are at about 40 percent. There are no intermediate elimination goals for the IRBMs—the only requirement is that at the end of three years all the missiles be gone.

I will conclude here. A very obvious and not terribly profound conclusion, I suppose I could make, is that we are one year into a 13-year relationship. This is not the time for euphoric predictions. The experiences of this last year do, however, allow us to be optimistic about onsite inspection. But we must also remember what it does not do. Onsite inspection is only one tool in verifying this treaty. By far the more crucial capability remains the National Technical Means, which provide us an overwatch of the entire Soviet Union. I can only bring my inspectors to those facilities listed in the MOU and compare what I find with what is contained in the MOU. I can tell you with great certitude what is going on and what is not going on at those specific sites. But it is only one view.

The onsite inspection process will give us more contact, more knowledge, more mutual understanding, and hopefully more predictability in our relationship. This in itself is, to my mind, a very positive development.

5

Whither Conventional Arms Control?

Paul Doty

We are far closer to substantially reducing military forces in Europe in ways that will improve security and lower costs than I would have thought possible when I spoke here two years ago. Progress toward this goal has been especially marked in the last five months. Hence, this is a timely occasion to take measure of what has happened and to look ahead.

NEW INITIATIVES IN CONVENTIONAL ARMS CONTROL

A number of seminal changes have converged to make possible a new political and military relation between East and West. One is the increasing realization of how much it costs to maintain the present military confrontation in a time when so many other needs cry for attention. The worldwide cost of military forces now exceeds a trillion dollars per year. To put this in perspective: the poorer half of the world lives on roughly this amount. Moreover, half of this trillion dollars is spent in Europe to support year after year the greatest concentration of military forces ever assembled in peacetime. Clearly, if both sides perceive that threats have declined, then the way becomes open to maintain defenses at lower levels of military forces.

After three years of revolutionary change in the Soviet Union, the basis of the West's fears is eroding. As a member of the Central Committee told a group of us who visited Moscow recently: "The Cold War is over. You have won. You have contained us except for a few excursions from which we are now retreating. You kept the real left from coming to power in Western Europe. We are relaxing our influence in Eastern Europe. We are no longer your enemy. The time has come to build a new relationship." While the West may not want to embrace instantly this exuberant view, evidence supporting it is accumulating. The withdrawal from Afghanistan has been the most obvious instance. A number of Gorbachev's proposals in arms control have set the stage for serious negotiation: the most crucial have been the enlargement of the realm for negotiations from central Europe to the Atlantic-to-the-Urals region, asymmetric reductions to reach parity and advocating very deep cuts, and a restructuring of armed forces to defensive postures. In the realm of action the unilateral cuts in Soviet military forces proposed last December are already under way and will substantially reduce the surprise attack capability of the Warsaw Pact. Yet it is not enough to say that the Cold War is over. Rather these changes have created the opportunity to reduce and restructure armed forces on both sides to conform with its being over. This is the challenge to be met.

Perhaps the most important development favoring substantial military reductions is the Soviet Union's acceptance of a remarkable degree of openness. This in turn has made verification of reductions in military forces possible for the first time. The shift began with the Stockholm Agreement of 1986, which provided for notification of military movements, for viewing each side's field exercises and for some onsite inspection of forces. The implementation of this agreement has gone extremely well. Next came the Intermediate Range Nuclear Force (INF) Treaty, which involved detailed verification of the destruction of major weapons systems. This too has proceeded in an exemplary fashion.

Finally, there is the rapidly developing drive toward unification in Western Europe. As Europe moves toward a broader identity it is playing a larger role in planning for military reductions and seeking a more positive role in Eastern Europe. Substantial negotiated reductions of NATO and Warsaw Pact forces could provide a way out of the endless "burden-sharing" arguments that torment NATO. That is, responsible military reductions could allow both the withdrawal of some U.S. forces from Europe and some reduction in Western European forces, while modifying somewhat the role of each. For example, the United States could maintain its support and resupply role and reduce its combat strength while the European allies increased where necessary their active or reserve forces.

THE END OF THE BEGINNING

Given these unusual motivations, how have the negotiations progressed? Planning began in November 1986 for two sets of conventional arms control negotiations to start not later than January 1989 in Vienna. These sessions were part of a larger forum based on the Helsinki Final Act of 1975, whereby three areas are considered together: security, economic cooperation, and human rights. One of the two planning efforts was aimed at producing a negotiating plan—a mandate—to achieve further transparency of peacetime military operations. Conducted by the members of NATO, the Warsaw Pact, and the neutrals in Europe (a total of 35 nations), this effort and the subsequent negotiations go by the awkward name of the *Conference on Confidence and Security-Building Measures and Disarmament in Europe*, or CSBM (or CDE) for short. This is the body that produced the Stockholm Agreement in 1986.

The other planning effort, a much more ambitious one, dealt with negotiating the reduction of troops and major equipment such as tanks, artillery, and armored troop carriers in the Atlantic-to-the-Urals region. This will proceed in Vienna in parallel with the CSBM talks and will be known as the *Negotiations on Conventional Armed Forces in Europe*, or CFE, which stands for Conventional Forces in Europe. All the member states of NATO and the Warsaw Pact, 23 in all, would participate in this negotiation. With some difficulty France was included, even though she insists on remaining militarily independent of NATO.

These planning negotiations moved forward in a slow and labored fashion during most of the two-year time period set for them. The United States, Britain, and Canada held out for major concessions on human rights agreements. Each side had to prepare a comprehensive list of equipment subject to reductions. Initially, NATO appeared to doubt that the Soviets, who provide the majority of forces for the Pact, would negotiate away their more than 2:1 numerical advantage in tanks, artillery, and armored troop carriers, so-called asymmetries. Consequently, internal NATO discussions focused on how to bring about asymmetrical reductions to reach common ceilings. In contrast, the Soviets made known their preference for a much broader three-stage plan that would first reduce asymmetries to the level of the side having the lower total in each major category, then reduce both sides by 500,000 personnel and equipment and, in the third stage, restructure the forces so as to be unambiguously in a defensive posture, incapable of large-scale offensive action. Clearly, an agreement on the inventory of relevant weapons would be essential to forward movement in the negotiations—hence the concern over whether the data to be presented by the two sides would show reasonable agreement.

Just as NATO was about to announce its count of its own weapons and its estimate of those of the Warsaw Pact, General Secretary Gorbachev startled the West by proposing on 7 December 1988, that the Soviet Union would sharply reduce its armed forces:

> Within the next two years their numerical strength will be reduced by 500,000 men. The numbers of conventional armaments will also be reduced. This will be done unilaterally, without relation to the talks on the mandate of the Vienna meeting.

Many, but not all, details were spelled out. In the Atlantic-to-the-Urals region, 240,000 personnel would be removed, along with 10,000 tanks, 8,500 artillery, and 800 aircraft. Most important, within these totals, 6 tank divisions, 50,000 troops, and a total of 5,300 tanks would be withdrawn from Central Europe and disbanded. This reduction amounts to more than a quarter of the Soviet tanks and 10 percent of the artillery in Central Europe. Although the Pact retains a 2:1 tank advantage, it sufficiently thins out their force so as to make an attack without prior reinforcement virtually impossible. Moreover, Eastern European governments have subsequently announced plans for reducing their armed forces by 46,000 men and 1,700 tanks. These moves constitute the most impressive unilateral step taken since the end of World War II. Its most important effect has been to convince most skeptics that the Soviet Union is seriously interested in large-scale disarmament in the Atlantic-to-the-Urals region. Marshall Akhromeyev told us in January that, although he was originally opposed to unilateral cuts, he came to support them because it was the only way to inject movement into the Vienna negotiations, to indicate their clear intent, and to begin saving resources for other uses at home.

NATO announced its count of conventional forces on December 8 and the Warsaw Pact followed on January 30. Since the two sides defined categories differently, as might have been expected, many comparisons could not be made directly. For example, NATO counted only artillery of 100-millimeter bore or larger; the Warsaw Pact included all artillery and even mortars. In aircraft the Pact assigned many more NATO types to their category of "ground-attack aircraft" than for their own, thereby implying that NATO has a superiority in relevant aircraft numbers. In fact the Warsaw Pact has a 1.85:1 advantage in total military aircraft in the region by Western counts. Nevertheless, taking this into account the tallies are mostly within reasonable agreement, although much remains to be done to reach agreement using common definitions of categories. Thus, the situation has come a long way since two years ago when the Soviet Union insisted that there was near equality in tanks. According to NATO data, the Warsaw Pact advantage, including stored NATO tanks, is 2.2; using Warsaw Pact data the advantage is 1.94.

OPENING POSITIONS

By mid-January 1989 all disputes—now mostly intraalliance disagreement—had been resolved. Agreements reached in Vienna covered not only the mandates for the CFE and CSBM conventional arms negotiations but also important agreements on human rights, terrorism, scientific cooperation, trade, travel, and freedom of information—an important advance over the original Helsinki Final Act of 1975. The foreign ministers met on January 16 to sign the agreements. Sandwiched between news of the Lybian chemical weapons plant and the coming inauguration, the American press scarcely covered this historic event that portends so much for Europe and East-West relations. German press reports speak of the first redesigning of the European political landscape since the Yalta Conference of 1945.

The CFE and CSBM negotiations began on March 6. The principal features of each side's opening positions are already clear. Despite some major differences, there is a great deal of common ground on the central issue—setting equal ceilings on the major conventional weapons and setting these ceilings somewhat below that of the lower inventory, which is almost always that of NATO. This will be the centerpiece of any future agreement. Moreover, there seems to be wide agreement on the need for intensive verification measures and the establishment of a common data base in order to determine what cuts have to be made.

The NATO proposal puts a cap on tanks, artillery, and armored troop carriers at 90 to 95 percent of present NATO levels for both sides. This position imposes much more severe cuts on the Warsaw Pact but simply in proportion to their present advantage. The Soviet position is to reduce these levels somewhat more and to include helicopters and ground-attack aircraft, or "strike aircraft" to use their term, since, as they recall from the German invasion, aircraft can decide the outcome of many land battles. NATO opposes the inclusion of aircraft for several reasons. Philosophically, they insist that the weapons of first concern are those used to capture and hold territory: aircraft do not fit this definition. The Soviet attempt to define a class of aircraft whose primary capability is to support ground forces seems unlikely to survive because so many types of aircraft can in an emergency serve in this mission. Moreover, such a restriction would eliminate many NATO aircraft that are configured for nuclear mission, an area not covered by conventional forces talks. Finally, the French are adamantly opposed to any aircraft restriction. Clearly this will be a difficult point to resolve. Further, the ability of each side to introduce aircraft from beyond the Atlantic-to-the-Urals region will have to be considered. Since it would be unreasonable to forego the benefits of reaching low-level parity on the major land weapons to avoid restricting aircraft that are already present in nearly equal numbers, some kind of agreement restricting aircraft will be reached.

The NATO position also calls for restricting the major force equipment that any one country can station in another to 30 percent of the total in that country. Since Soviet Union forces dominate the Warsaw Pact posture, such a restriction seems biased against the Soviet Union, but taking into account that several countries may host Soviet forces, it might be negotiable. Both sides recognize the need to proceed through the creation of zones beginning in the central region in order to facilitate verification and reduce further the likelihood of surprise attack. However, the definitions and functioning of such zones are quite different in the two proposals.

Finally, the two positions differ in overall scope. The NATO proposal focuses on reaching parity at levels slightly below the lower current inventory. The Soviet position—no actual proposal has been tabled—emphasizes the three stages mentioned above in which first-stage reductions are to 85 to 90 percent of the lowest level currently possessed by either side, followed by a further 25 percent or more reduction in the second stage, and a transition to defensive military postures in the third stage. This more comprehensive plan paints a larger, more attractive picture. A number of individuals and groups have advocated extending the NATO position in this direction. Congressman Aspin has urged that NATO aim at substantially lower ceilings than 95 percent of the current lower level. Leading military figures share this position. General Goodpaster, in a current report, goes further and urges "consideration of a radical restructuring of the forces of NATO and the Warsaw Pact, on the basis of parity, with active forces on each side at no more than 50 percent of the present NATO strength" by 1995. Similar recommendations for deeper cuts are being made unofficially on the Soviet side as well. These suggestions would carry the negotiation well into the second stage of the Soviet proposal and require substantial restructuring of forces and doctrine mentioned above.

OBSTACLES AND HOPE

Deep reductions will force a profound recasting of not only military doctrine and force structure but also of traditional public and governmental attitudes as well. This, in turn, will create an opportunity to move toward convincing defensive postures that would greatly reduce the threat in Central Europe. But many barriers lie in the way. For example, a tenet of military thought has been that the progressive thinning out of forces along a dividing line—technically as the "force-to-space" ratio is reduced—a point will be reached when defense against a concentrated attack from the other side cannot be sustained. Many believe that this point would be reached along the inter-German border if the current troop strength were reduced much below 85 percent of NATO's present force. Then the front could not be continuously covered and forces would have to be reconfigured into much more maneuverable, independently operating units. Nevertheless, alternatives do exist. For example, close air support and the construction of barriers near the inter-German border would provide substantial compensation for the thinning of troop strength. Long opposed by the West Germans, barriers will become more important if forward defense is to be maintained while troops are withdrawn. In short, the threshold at about 85 percent of current NATO strength is not a line that cannot be crossed but rather the point at which new conceptions of defense and drastic restructuring of forces and doctrine must begin to take over.

Before real progress can be made, the two sides must resolve the difficult and detailed problems of negotiating a common data base and agreeing on the verification methodology that will ensure that both sides are in compliance with what is agreed. Such an effort is certain to be very labor intensive and will clearly involve many military officers. Training military personnel for this task along with intensive language preparation will probably be the first sign that real work is under way.

The difficult job of verification will be greatly aided by the development of new verification technology. Many existing sensors designed for combat can be adapted to the kind of surveillance needed for verification. The use of overflights and observers at road and rail junctions and with military units to be disbanded will be needed in an expanded verification regime.

A related development can be seen in the rapid growth of computer modeling that is under way. Modeling to compare the capabilities of conventional forces and the outcomes of engagements have been widespread for some time. Their relevance is often questioned because the outcome of any conflict depends on so many nonquantifiable variables— leadership, training, readiness, morale, logistics, geography, weather, civilian cooperation, and more—that no program dependent on numerical variables can hope to predict success or failure. However, modeling can be useful in making comparisons where the nonquantifiable variables are assumed to remain unchanged, for example, in comparing the consequences of alternative reduction regimes.

In this spirit a meeting is being held this week in which several Soviet and American experts will compare their programs and results for simple comparison cases. As an example of progress along these lines, Dr. Epstein of the Brookings Institution has just developed his own dynamic model to the point where it can compare the relative advantage to each side of the current arms control proposals using a variety of attack scenarios. Whether different computer programs will lead to similar conclusions is clearly of interest.

THE OUTLOOK

In two years it should be possible to see if this ambitious program is moving toward fruition. This is the period in which the Soviet unilateral reductions are to be carried out. And the negotiators must report to the Conference on Security and Cooperation in Europe, the permanent body that carries forward the Helsinki Final Act.

This period should be a most exciting one. In terms of weapons, we will see whether the Soviet unilateral withdrawals will continue on the way to a low-level parity across the East-West divide in Europe. The political accompaniment will be rich and diverse. We will see if the Soviet Union sacrifices its presently declared intent of seeking deep cuts in European forces to the quite different goals of breaking up NATO or separating the United States from Europe. And we will see if Eastern Europe can evolve toward more democratic forms of government without putting the security of the Soviet Union at risk. We will see if NATO can broaden its position to present a more far-reaching vision of how a much reduced and defensively postured military confrontation can contribute to "the common home of Europe" and to the broad easing of East-West tensions.

Because of the complexity of this radical change in the military confrontation, we must be ready for setbacks. Nevertheless, if a review two years hence shows that there has been more failure than accomplishment, hope might still arise from a different quarter: the Stockholm agreements might by then be greatly extended in the separate CSBM negotiations, so that a disengagement of forces could be choreographed in a quite different fashion. This negotiation could possibly produce agreements on surveillance, repositioning of forces to the rear, and limits on the size of exercises that would greatly enhance European security well before actual force reductions reached parity. Furthermore, it may turn out that reductions of troops and weapons by means of a series of reciprocal steps similar to the Soviet unilateral initiative of last December might be undertaken if the present plans prove too cumbersome. At present this kind of outcome seems quite fanciful because the Western position is to deal only with limited extensions of the Stockholm Agreement until parity in force reductions is reached. But it is clear that the path to negotiated parity will be long and hard. Even if the willingness to compromise is there, the effort could bog down over the complexity of the problem or the difficulties inherent in negotiating with 23 or 35 delegations.

Thus, the direct approach in the CFE negotiations deserves full, committed support. But we have no experience in disassembling the greatest war machines ever built: this may require repeated attempts and some trial and error approaches to bring it off. So, much innovation, resourcefulness, and patience will be needed. But the most urgent need is for the political will, backed by an informed public, to ensure that this remarkable opening is turned to mankind's advantage.

By 1995, 50 years will have passed since the end of World War II. The postwar period will be over, and a new kind of world order will begin to shape the next 50 years. If that new order is to deal effectively with the towering challenges of the next century, much of the current investment in military confrontation will have to give way to cooperation and even partnership. Arms control is only one of several tools that can make this grand transition possible, but what is done with this tool in the next few years will be decisive to the outcome.

NOTE ADDED IN PROOF: Following this presentation, the Soviet Union on 25 May 1989 agreed to the limits on tanks and armored personnel carriers in the central region that had been suggested by NATO. On May 30 President Bush announced that NATO would remove much of the remaining difference in positions by agreeing to include troop reductions and combat aircraft in the CFE negotiations. Specifically he proposed that U.S. troops be reduced by 30,000 as part of reduction of U.S. and Soviet troops stationed in Europe to a common ceiling of 275,000, that combat aircraft and helicopters be reduced to 15 percent below current Alliance holdings, and that all withdrawn equipment be destroyed. These new proposals will be tabled in detail in Vienna in September 1989.

6

Prospects for a Chemical Weapons Disarmament Treaty

Matthew Meselson

After 20 years of discussion and negotiation in Geneva in the 40-nation Conference on Disarmament and its predecessor bodies, recent developments may result in a chemical disarmament treaty ready for signing within a year or two. Chief among these developments are Soviet acceptance of U.S. verification concepts, increased international concern with proliferation, and the support of President Bush.

The emerging Chemical Weapons Convention bans the development, production, possession, and transfer of chemical weapons, under a system of international onsite verification. Antichemical protective activities and equipment, such as gas masks, are permitted.

Three categories of chemical warfare agents are stocked by the United States and the USSR: the highly lethal organophosphorus nerve agents, first produced but not used by Germany during World War II; blister agents dating from World War I; and an irritant or riot-control agent introduced in the 1950s. Iraq, the only other nation that admits having chemical weapons, used blister and probably nerve agents in the Gulf War. According to recent congressional testimony by the director of

Central Intelligence, as many as 20 countries may be developing chemical weapons.

Under common meteorological conditions, approximately 1 ton of nerve agent or approximately 10 tons of blister agent is sufficient to cause heavy casualties to unprotected personnel within a square kilometer and additional casualties downwind. The delivery of 1 ton of nerve agent by 155-millimeter artillery, for example, would require firing some 300 projectiles. This makes nerve agents competitive with or superior to conventional high-explosive munitions for the attack of troops lacking antichemical protection.

The situation is reversed, however, if the target personnel are wearing gas masks and protective clothing. Soldiers wearing such protective gear are far less vulnerable to chemicals than they are to conventional high-explosive and flame weapons. For direct casualty production, therefore, it would generally be wasteful of effort and ammunition to deploy and deliver chemicals rather than conventional munitions. And, of course, chemical weapons cannot directly disable or destroy tanks, other combat vehicles, artillery, or other equipment or installations.

Instead of casualty production, the principal effect of chemical weapons against troops wearing antichemical protection is to slow them down and reduce their efficiency. At high work rates in hot weather, the retention of body heat imposed by the suit, mask, and gloves forces the wearer to limit heavy exertion to short intervals or else to partly open the protective clothing. Even in cool weather the wearing of a mask and gloves causes some impairment of vision, speech intelligibility, and dexterity.

The issue relevant to evaluating the combat utility of chemical weapons against an adversary with good antichemical protection and training is the degree to which one's use of chemical weapons degrades the combat effectiveness of the other side by causing him to enter or intensify an antichemical protective posture. This is difficult to assess realistically. Degradation is substantial for dismounted troops strenuously engaged in hot weather or for units poorly trained to operate in antichemical protection. In contrast, field exercises with well-trained personnel in temperate weather show little degradation of unit mission performance.

A serious concern in the combat use of chemical weapons is the hazard to unprotected civilians downwind of target areas. Depending on meteorological, terrain, and other factors, one may calculate, for example, that unless provided with masks or protective shelters, hundreds of thousands or millions of civilians could be killed in a few days of general nerve gas operations in a region with a population distribution like that of Central Europe. A further concern, heightened by the continued proliferation of chemical weapons and their use in the Gulf War, is the threat they could pose to civilians as weapons of terror.

The objective of the Chemical Weapons Convention being negotiated in Geneva is to replace the present situation in which there is no international prohibition against possession of chemical weapons and in which an increasing number of nations have or are seeking such weapons with an effective global ban. The convention is now in an advanced phase of negotiation. There is general agreement on most of the major conceptual issues and on many of the technical details, as reflected in a "rolling text" of the draft convention of some 100 pages.

The convention will be implemented by a permanent Organization for the Prohibition of Chemical Weapons, somewhat like the International Atomic Energy Agency. At the outset of the convention, its states parties must declare to the international organization the precise locations and detailed makeup of their stocks of chemical weapons and agents and the facilities for their production, development, and testing. The declared stocks and facilities will then be verified and eliminated according to a prescribed schedule over a period of 10 years.

A primary task of the international organization is to operate a three-tier system of verification. First, its inspectors will inventory and seal all declared stocks and declared chemical weapons production facilities and will monitor their nondiversion and ultimate destruction. Second, the international organization will operate a system of short-notice inspection and data collection intended to verify that chemical weapons are not produced within the chemical industry. Third, as a safety net to deal with suspicious activities and to deter violations, there will be short-notice challenge inspections at the request of a state party, with no right of refusal by the requested state.

Verification of the nonproduction of chemical weapons is facilitated by the fact that there is no substantial peaceful use for any of the most threatening chemical warfare agents, such as the nerve and blister agents, or for the organophosphorus precursors contained in binary nerve agent weapons. The convention prohibits the production of these substances except for small quantities, restricted to research, medical, or protective purposes. The convention further requires that facilities producing, processing, or consuming more than limited quantities of certain chemicals with peaceful uses that are also key precursors of chemical warfare agents be declared and placed under a system of monitoring and short-notice inspection to verify that such facilities and precursors are not diverted to weapons purposes.

Verification of nonproduction of prohibited substances and nondiversion of key precursors to weapons purposes will be based on examination of plant design and records, on data from tamper-proof monitoring devices, and on chemical analysis of appropriate samples. Such procedures are probably capable of detecting the production or presence of prohibited substances at a facility even if there have been determined cleanup efforts. Actual tests of this expectation, however, are only now under way.

Verification to safeguard against production, stockpiling, and other prohibited activities at undeclared sites and facilities will depend on challenge inspection. Initial detection would depend on national intelligence means and other sources of information, possibly including information that may come into the possession of the international organization. Even uncertain indication of prohibited activities at a particular site could trigger a request by a state party for challenge inspection. In order to form some idea of how large an undeclared chemical stockpile must be to have military significance, it may be noted that unclassified estimates of the U.S. stockpile in Germany, said to be adequate for only a few days of chemical operations by U.S. forces in Europe, place it at some 400–500 tons of nerve agent, contained in about 6,500 tons of munitions, or approximately 100,000 artillery projectiles.

Given the value of short-notice challenge inspection, both in evaluating suspicious activities and as a deterrent to cheating, the United States would probably exercise its challenge inspection rights regularly even in cases where no suspicions exist, in order to keep the political threshold for challenge inspections low and their deterrent effect high. This has been the practice in requests for challenge inspections of troop exercises in Europe under the 1986 Stolkholm Agreement on Confidence and Security Building Measures in Europe.

This abbreviated discussion of verification issues may be concluded by emphasizing that while there can be no absolute assurance against prohibited activities, the verification provisions of the convention, together with national intelligence means and other sources of information, would create a serious risk of detection and exposure of any substantial violation.

For the United States the principal benefits of the Chemical Weapons Convention are, first, the verified elimination of large stocks in the Soviet Union, which they have declared to total some 50,000 tons of nerve, blister, and irritant agents, in weapons and in bulk. A second substantial benefit would be the creation of a strong international legal and political norm prohibiting chemical weapons, together with a verification regime to deter violations and to combat chemical proliferation.

The principal cost of the convention to the United States is the loss of its present option to have chemical weapons for deterrence and for retaliation in kind, specifically in the defense of Europe. But a number of factors make U.S. chemical weapons of dubious utility for European defense. Soviet forces are well equipped with antichemical protective equipment and well trained in its use. Key NATO allies are reluctant to integrate chemical weapons into overall defense planning and several have formally renounced the option of having or using them. In March the chancellor of the Federal Republic of Germany (FRG), Helmut Kohl, predicted that there will be chemical disarmament, saying, "We will do everything to make these weapons disappear, because we do not need them." By agreement with the FRG, U.S. chemical weapons in Germany, the only U.S. stocks in Europe, although in excellent condition, will soon be withdrawn and will not be replaced.

If the United States forgoes its chemical weapons option as the result of a chemical weapons disarmament treaty, the maintenance of a strong antichemical defense would nevertheless be necessary. Antichemical defense is an essential adjunct to the Chemical Weapons Convention. First, it reduces incentives for cheating. Second, a good defense enhances the effectiveness of verification, by increasing the scale of preparations necessary to achieve military significance. Finally, antichemical defense is a safeguard in case of any actual use of chemical weapons. To protect defensive programs, the Administration would seek and the Congress would undoubtedly mandate a number of safeguards, such as permanent status for the Army Chemical Corps and budget priority for maintaining and improving antichemical defense.

While these and other issues continue to be studied and debated, the prevailing view in the Administration and in the Senate is favorable to a

Chemical Weapons Convention. President Bush has frequently voiced his commitment to the elimination of chemical weapons. In his foreign policy address at the University of Toledo during the presidential campaign, he said, "If I am remembered for anything, it would be this: a complete and total ban on chemical weapons." After the election the President reaffirmed his commitment in his address to the joint session of Congress in February and at the NATO summit in May when he said: "We must achieve a global chemical weapons ban as quickly as possible."

In June, 75 senators, including a majority of both political parties, sent a letter to President Bush declaring their "strong support for your personal commitment to ridding the world of chemical weapons." The Board of Directors of the U.S. Chemical Manufacturers Association, representing nearly the entire U.S. chemical industry, also has declared its support for a chemicals disarmament treaty, and the association is working with the U.S. Government to develop verification procedures and with industry groups in other countries to achieve a common international approach to the problem.

Since the summer of 1987, when the Soviets first agreed to the concept of mandatory challenge inspection, they have seemed genuinely eager to have a verified global ban on chemical weapons. An important test of their priorities, and of U.S. priorities too, will be the outcome of current U.S.-Soviet talks aimed at exchanging detailed information regarding their respective stocks and initiating bilateral inspections, including challenge inspections, even before the convention is signed. The objective is to test procedures and build mutual confidence in the accuracy of declarations, especially because the size given by the Soviet Union for its stockpile has been said by U.S. and British officials to be considerably less than Western intelligence estimates.

An indicator of worldwide attitudes to the convention is the January 1989 Declaration of the Paris Conference on the Prohibition of Chemical Weapons, called by Presidents Reagan and Mitterrand. Although the principal Islamic nations of the Middle East argue for a link between chemical disarmament and progress toward nuclear disarmament in their region, these nations and indeed all of the 149 nations represented at the conference joined in the final declaration calling for urgent efforts to conclude the convention at the earliest date, making no reference to other issues. With the expected admission of Iraq, Israel, Libya, and Syria, nearly all of the confrontation states of the Middle East will be participating in the future negotiation of the convention in Geneva, either as original members of the Conference on Disarmament or as observers.

Numerous important issues must be resolved before the convention can be ready for signing. Among these are (1) the rules and safeguards for challenge inspections; (2) the system for selecting facilities for inspection to verify nonproduction of chemical weapons in the chemical industry; (3) the membership of the executive council of the international organization; and (4) provisions to ensure general adherence, particularly of third world nations. While solutions to these and other problems remain to be devised, agreed, and cast into treaty language, the main outlines of the Chemical Weapons Convention are in place and, given sufficient priority by the United States and USSR, a ban on chemical weapons is likely.

7

Vitality of the Nuclear Nonproliferation Treaty Regime

Spurgeon M. Keeny, Jr.

I

The United States has opposed the proliferation of nuclear weapons to other countries since the beginning of the nuclear age in 1945. Over the years, however, the priority given to this policy has varied when it came into conflict with other U.S. foreign policy objectives.

Today, the highest arms control priority clearly should be directed to early completion of a START treaty in order to control and reduce the immense U.S.-Soviet nuclear arsenals, which could destroy civilization. But the spread of nuclear weapons to additional countries possibly presents the greater danger that nuclear weapons might actually be used, if only on a small scale. In the long term, with improved U.S.-Soviet relations, widespread nuclear proliferation, with greater possibility of use, could become the greater threat to U.S. and world security. Even small numbers of nuclear weapons in the hands of fanatical or unstable nations increases the likelihood of irresponsible use of these weapons. Such use could, by design or accident, draw the major powers into regional conflicts involving nuclear weapons, which in turn could lead to general nuclear war.

Fortunately, our priority interest in the START treaty with the Soviet Union and our nonproliferation policy are not in conflict but actually reinforce each other.

II

Over the past few years a great deal of information has become publicly available on the advanced state of nuclear weapons programs in Israel, Pakistan, India, and South Africa. So far these countries have denied possession of nuclear weapons and have let their adversaries and the rest of the world speculate on the actual status of their nuclear capabilities. On occasion they have stimulated these speculations by well-placed, provocative, unofficial leaks. Throughout the world concern has increased that one or more of these countries will decide to come out of the closet and officially proclaim their possession of nuclear weapons.

Coming at this time, this latest nuclear proliferation crisis—and this is not the first—presents both a danger and an opportunity. It is a danger, since formal proclamation of their nuclear capabilities could initiate a domino effect of declarations by other closet nuclear weapons states at this time, breaking down the current international norm against nuclear proliferation.

Opportunity exists, since the United States, working with most of the rest of the world community that has accepted the present nonproliferation norm, has increased leverage in preventing this confrontation. In particular, Soviet withdrawal from Afghanistan should strengthen our hand with Pakistan. In addition, Israel's increasing isolation and internal problems should allow the United States to have increased influence on this critical issue, through quiet diplomacy.

III

Pursuing this nonproliferation policy, the United States can make use of an international nonproliferation regime, consisting of a complex of international treaties, regional agreements, domestic legislation, informal agreements, and bilateral and multilateral diplomatic initiatives. This regime, which has evolved over the past 45 years, probably has more vitality today than at any time in the past.

First and most important, the Nonproliferation Treaty, the NPT, signed in 1968, provides a framework for the regime. The NPT is based on a fundamental bargain: namely, nonnuclear weapons states agreed to renounce nuclear weapons in exchange for a pledge of the three original nuclear weapons states—the United States, the United Kingdom, and the Soviet Union—to share peaceful nuclear technology with them. This is really an extension of Eisenhower's original Atoms for Peace concept.

The nuclear weapons states also agreed to seek an end to the nuclear arms race. And all nonnuclear weapons state signatories agreed to place *all* of their nuclear facilities under "full scope" safeguards, operated by the IAEA, the International Atomic Energy Agency. These safeguards, which have been very successful, are designed not to prevent but rather to sound alarms if illegal activities (e.g., diversions of materials) are suspected at declared facilities.

There are now over 130 signatories to the NPT. Although the most threatening proliferators—Israel, Pakistan, India, and South Africa—have not joined the NPT, the treaty has nevertheless established international norms of nonproliferation that indirectly affect even the holdout states. Moreover, even though France has never formally signed the NPT, it now, in practice, conforms with the treaty. China, also a nonsignatory, has increasingly conformed with the treaty's objectives.

Second, regional nuclear free zones reinforce the NPT. The Latin America Nuclear Free Zone, created by the Treaty of Tlatelolco, which was signed in 1968 though not fully in force, has served to help exclude nuclear weapons from Latin America. A protocol to this treaty, which has been signed by all five nuclear powers—the only such document in existence—commits them to respect the nonnuclear nature of the zone. By other agreements, nuclear weapons are also excluded by treaty from Antarctica and, potentially, from the South Pacific.

Third, the regime is further reinforced by export controls, both informal and by statute. Every major nuclear supplier has informally agreed to guidelines on sensitive nuclear equipment which they will not export to other countries without IAEA safeguards.

The United States has also restricted exports of sensitive equipment by domestic legislation. In 1978 the U.S. Nuclear Nonproliferation Act called for tighter safeguards on exports than those imposed by the NPT, in an attempt to discourage the plutonium fuel cycle in commercial reactors. This fuel cycle, which cannot now be justified on economic grounds, would create large inventories of plutonium, and thereby establish a base for a relatively rapid breakout to a weapons program, as well as increase the possibilities of diversions.

The U.S. Congress has also enacted legislation prohibiting economic or military assistance to nations supplying or receiving nonsafeguarded uranium enrichment or plutonium reprocessing equipment. But under pressure of the conflicting priorities of U.S. support for Pakistan in connection with the Afghanistan war, the Administration and Congress backed off from implementing these provisions in the face of clear Pakistani violations. However, this matter is still open, and additional legislation has been passed specific to Pakistan, denying future aid—military and economic aid—unless the President certifies that Pakistan does not possess a nuclear explosive device. In addition, separate legislation, which the President cannot override on national security grounds, requires the cutting off of all aid to any nonnuclear weapons state that tests a nuclear weapon.

Fourth, and often overlooked, is the fact that over the years the United States has exerted quiet pressure, which has often been quite effective, on various states not to pursue the nuclear weapons option. The most successful examples were South Korea and Taiwan, which in the 1970s were persuaded to abandon some nascent nuclear weapons ambitions.

In the case of South Africa, multinational diplomatic efforts undoubtedly discouraged its nuclear-test program, after a test site was discovered by a Soviet satellite in 1977 in the Kalahari Desert. In this connection I should note that reports that South Africa subsequently detonated a nuclear device in the South Atlantic are not supported by the facts.

In the case of Israel and Pakistan, while discouraging their nuclear ambitions, the United States has not used the full force of its considerable influence on either Pakistan or Israel to this end.

IV

Under this regime I believe the overall assessment is that nuclear nonproliferation has been remarkably effective. Looking back, one recalls government and academic predictions that by now there would be a large number of nuclear states—25 or more. In the first 20 years, however, since the beginning of the nuclear age in 1945, there were only four additional states: the Soviet Union, the United Kingdom, France, and

China. This initial proliferation was probably inevitable, given the existing political situation.

In the next 25 years, since 1965, only one additional state has tested a nuclear device, and that is India. Significantly, India insisted at the time, and since, that its test was for peaceful purposes (such as excavation)—then a more popular concept than today—and subsequently, apparently, did not vigorously pursue its weapons program.

Moreover, 10 to 15 years ago, if I were to have given a list of states with clear nuclear ambitions, it would have included eight states. In addition to the present four, I would have included Argentina, Brazil, South Korea, and Taiwan. But today the latter four states have probably abandoned their immediate nuclear weapons operations, although future changes in the governments in Argentina and Brazil could reopen this problem.

Although the present four states—Israel, Pakistan, India, and South Africa—are obviously much further along today than they were 10 or 15 years ago, they are not new threats to the regime. Israel has been engaged in its program for at least three decades, India has been engaged in its for at least two decades, and Pakistan for some 15 years.

Above all, it is also important to remember that not only the overwhelming majority of states but also such industrial giants as Germany and Japan have decided that their security is best served by remaining nonnuclear weapons states.

V

I will say a word about the Israeli and Pakistani programs, which time prevents me from discussing in detail. Let me emphasize that these comments are not intended to diminish or dismiss the seriousness of the continuation of these programs but rather to keep them in perspective.

I would observe that both countries officially insist that they do not possess nuclear weapons. Both countries also clearly have made a major effort to develop nuclear weapons programs and have engaged in extensive programs of espionage over the years to accomplish this objective. Both countries also, unofficially, seek to build up the international image of the effectiveness and significance of their programs.

In the case of Israel the revelations by Mordecai Vanunu in England, before he was kidnapped and taken back to Israel for trial, in late 1986 suggest a larger and more advanced program than most informed observers had assumed previously. One now hears estimates that Israel's capability to deploy, or deploy on short notice, nuclear devices might be between 50 and 200, based on availability of material. This compares with earlier estimates that might be closer to 25. I would, myself, guess that the truth lies at the lower end of the new scale. But this is still a very significant capability. I also do not believe the evidence supports the claims that the Israelis are stockpiling untested thermonuclear weapons, in the sense that we would define a thermonuclear weapon. Nevertheless, Israel clearly has a significant program and can presumably deliver these weapons, both by aircraft obtained from the United States and by their own Jericho II ballistic missiles.

As for the Pakistani program, there is pretty clear evidence, publicly available, that they have or could assemble on short notice a few simple nuclear devices, presumably employing enriched uranium from the centrifuge enrichment plant at Kahuta. The Pakistan weapons program has reached the point where the Administration has warned Congress that it will probably not be able to furnish the required statutory finding this year that Pakistan does not have a weapons capability.

VI

What is to be done? Since Israel, India, South Africa, and even Pakistan now have extensive indigenous technical capabilities, there are limits to what the United States or the international community can do. Nevertheless, let me suggest the most obvious actions we can and should take within the existing nonproliferation regime.

First, the United States and the Soviet Union should sign the START agreement, if possible, before the next NPT five-year review conference in 1990. Without fail, they must sign, ratify, and take major steps toward implementation of a START treaty well in advance of the 1995 NPT 25th anniversary conference, at which, according to the terms of the treaty, the future duration of the treaty will have to be decided. By demonstrating their good faith in meeting their NPT commitment to nuclear arms reductions, the superpowers can help ensure a strong endorsement for the indefinite, or at least long-duration, extension of a framework treaty upon which the nonproliferation regime rests.

Second, the United States should work to bring South Africa into the NPT, which South Africa has suggested it may be prepared to do. The United States should press the Soviet Union to get Cuba to join the Latin

America Nuclear Free Zone since this is necessary to bring the treaty into full force, ensuring coverage of the Argentine and Brazilian programs. I hope that Mr. Gorbachev's relations with Fidel Castro are sufficiently good to make this possible.

The United States should press Israel and Pakistan to stay in the closet and not confront neighbors with a declared nuclear weapons status that would be seen by their neighbors as requiring them to develop a chemical warfare response, which they could do in the relatively near future, and to preclude pressure on them to move to a nuclear weapons response in the more distant future.

To this end, we should (1) let Pakistan know that we will enforce the current legislation cutting off economic and military aid if Pakistan tests nuclear weapons, declares a nuclear status, or clearly possesses a nuclear weapons capability, and (2) let Israel know that a declared nuclear weapons status would necessitate a review of U.S. security policy toward Israel and that Israel would be subject to the same cutoff legislation as other countries if it conducts a nuclear weapons test.

Third, the United States should intensify work with other suppliers, including the Soviet Union and China, to tighten export controls on sensitive nuclear equipment and on delivery systems, such as long-range ballistic missiles, which make absolutely no sense except with nuclear warheads.

Fourth, and I would pursue the suggestion made by Roald Sagdeev, the United States and the Soviet Union should seek to expand the nonproliferation regime by negotiating a multinational comprehensive test ban and/ or a cutoff of fissionable materials for nuclear weapons. This would effectively answer criticisms of the discriminatory nature of the nonproliferation treaty bargain. Based on earlier statements, such treaties might be acceptable to India and other holdout states and would certainly put additional indirect pressure on them against declaring their nuclear status or attempting to carry out nuclear weapons tests.

Fifth, above all, we should work to defuse tensions in critical Mid-East and South Asian regions.

VII

In conclusion, I remain cautiously optimistic that with improved U.S.-Soviet relations it should be possible to hold the line on emerging nuclear weapons states. Even if in a moment of rash bravado or fear one or more of the present closet nuclear weapons states decides to announce officially its new status or to test nuclear weapons as a demonstration, cooperative efforts by the United States, the Soviet Union, and their allies should be sufficiently damage limiting to prevent a domino effect that would collapse the nonproliferation treaty regime.

But above all, in a practical sense, we must be certain that our actions, particularly in connection with the early completion of the START treaty, ensure that the NPT is extended in 1995, either indefinitely or for a prolonged period, so that the framework on which the nonproliferation regime is based will survive.

8

Summary Remarks

Marvin L. Goldberger

I am deeply disappointed in this panel because I had assumed that they would all talk so long that I would not have to say anything.

There are a lot of problems associated with trying to give a summary of these meetings. In the first place there is a kind of presumption that you all have a loss of short-term memory and that it is impaired to such an extent that a summary is necessary.

The second problem I had was to prepare my remarks in advance of having any serious knowledge of what some of the speakers were going to say, because I did not have their papers. In the course of trying to anticipate what they might say, I made various kinds of profound observations, most of which have now been said by these speakers.

A great deal has happened in the international security arena since we began this series of seminars in 1984. Among those things that have happened are Star Wars, Reykjavik, START, the INF Treaty, a new U.S. president, the flamboyant Mr. Gorbachev, with his perestroika, glasnost, and new thinking.

It is natural to ask the following kinds of questions: Are we moving into an entirely new era of arms control? Is the time ripe for dramatic cuts

72

in armaments, both nuclear and conventional? Is there real momentum provided by the unilateral steps taken by General Secretary Gorbachev? Is it possible that there has been a serious outbreak of rationality in the United States and the Soviet Union and Western Europe? If that is true, is there a way to make this disease spread to the Middle East, Asia, Africa, Latin America? Or will we wake up in a few months or years to find out it was all a beautiful dream and that little, if anything, has changed?

There is an inescapable sense in which one must say that we have not come closer to the core problem. There are over 50,000 nuclear weapons in the world, and the threat of a catastrophic war, with hundreds of millions of casualties, remains as the central issue of our time. We must not lose sight of that as we sort of painfully inch forward from the INF Treaty to START and to other steps of that variety.

Of course, the steps that we are talking about—START, conventional force reductions, and so on—are vitally important and highly desirable. But the implied threat of this obscene number of nuclear weapons remains terrifying, as long as there is even a tiny chance of their being used. It should hardly be necessary to tell this audience that the expected value—in this case the likely consequences of nuclear war—is the product of the destructive power of the weapons and the probability of their use. When you are talking about the explosive equivalent of about 10 billion tons of TNT, the probability of their being used had better be pretty damned small.

The fundamental issue is that we must stop thinking of nuclear weapons as anything other than things nations possess only to ensure that they never be used. They have no other rational value, and surely deterrence could be assured with a tenth or less of present arsenals. I think the point made last night by Mr. Woolsey that we must look forward to a time when nuclear weapons become boring, and consequently less preoccupying, is an objective that will help in trying to put them into proper perspective.

I want to recall briefly a few of the points made this morning by Professor Panofsky on the strategic arms problem. START is just a start, albeit a very important one. There are some serious issues, as he pointed out, that are holding up an agreement, primarily those related to decisions about mobile missiles, sea-launched cruise missiles, and, to some extent, the Strategic Defense Initiative (SDI).

The United States is objecting to the Soviet insistence on adherence to the ABM Treaty as signed for a period of 10 years, even though a sensible defense research program would scarcely feel any restrictions. Logically, the Russians should not be concerned because the forces that remain after a START agreement could render any conceivable defense impotent and obsolete (to quote from a famous saying). There is even some hope now that SDI might relax into a long-range research program, without the hype that has accompanied it up until now. At any rate, with hard work, it would seem that worries on both sides about START should be resolvable. Then we can address ourselves to the problem of radical strategic force reductions to a level that would require fundamental revisions of strategic doctrine and force structure.

CISAC, in studies to which Professor Panofsky referred this morning, has concluded that cuts by more than a factor of four would probably begin to trigger such reconsiderations and necessitate the inclusion of other nuclear powers in arms control discussions. When and if we reach such a regime, verification issues will grow in importance, and the experience that we are gaining in connection with the INF Treaty, which we heard about from General Lajoie, will be immensely helpful. I was very impressed by General Lajoie's presentation, and the thoroughness, effectiveness, and speed with which those steps have been put into practice.

I want to reemphasize another issue that came up briefly today, to which Roald Sagdeev, and also Spurgeon Keeny, referred. Mr. Gorbachev recently announced that the Soviet Union was going to stop the production of enriched uranium and was shutting down two plutonium weapons production reactors. The United States and Great Britain poohpoohed this, for reasons which I simply cannot understand. We have discussed, in others of this CISAC series of seminars, the idea of a complete halt in the production of fissionable materials for military purposes. This idea, incidentally, is quite old. It goes back to correspondence between Eisenhower and Bulganin in 1956. But it would seem the very opportunity to revive the idea in light of the Gorbachev initiatives.

Professor Sagdeev said a number of very important things this morning, raising the question of how we move away from this regime of overarming that has been dominant in the United States and the Soviet Union for so long. He also raised the issue that we do not seem to have an integrated overarching approach to arms control and disarmament, that we have tended to do things in a rather piecemeal fashion. First we have an INF Treaty, and then we have a strategic weapons treaty. We do various kinds of individual bean-counting operations. It is important to try to figure out where it is that we are going in a broader sense.

I was also very impressed by his comment that the Soviet Union has recognized now that it has made some errors in judgment in the past, that there have been some failures in their policy. We, too, have made some profound errors, which some people are a little reluctant to admit. For example, our decision to go ahead with multiple independently targetable reentry vehicles was clearly a mistake of the past. We, too, should emulate the Soviet Union, perhaps in recognition of mistakes of the past or just ab initio to consider what unilateral acts we could take that would stabilize the international scene.

The thrust of our afternoon discussion has been on things related to what you might term "good old war" and, to some extent, on old thinking. Modern technology has made even nonnuclear conflict potentially much more lethal and more impersonal than it was in World War II. Long-range ballistic missiles, small quiet submarines, chemical weapons production facilities, Stinger-like antiaircraft missiles, high-performance aircraft, and so on are being made by the industrial nations for each other and for their less well-developed friends who like to posture before real or imagined enemies. There is also a continuing effort in parts of the lesser developed countries to acquire that most macho of possessions, nuclear weapons. The little wars that are made possible by modern weaponry are often fueled by ancient religious or racial hatreds, and they have the potential, by virtue of their savagery and their geography, to draw in larger and stronger adversaries and pave the way for larger, and possibly nuclear, encounters.

This is a particularly important time for a reconsideration of the structure of conventional military forces in Europe. The proposals for unilateral reductions by the Soviet Union are of great political significance, and they may well be, in addition, militarily very significant. It is a little early to assess all of the implications, because some of the appropriate military responses depend upon the details of the proposed cuts. In the opinion of many students of this subject, if those unilateral steps are taken as promised, in an appropriate fashion, the bugaboo of a short-warning attack in Europe would disappear.

There is no doubt about the political response to the Gorbachev initiatives: It does not depend upon details, and Mr. Gorbachev has pulled off

76

another grand gesture that the Europeans cannot ignore. It is also likely that there will be political fallout in the United States related to budget problems and a growing weariness over the continued support of very affluent allies facing an apparently diminishing threat from the Soviet Union.

The current military forces in Europe are the product of almost 45 years of old thinking, based on ideological and political differences between NATO and the Warsaw Pact nations and, most particularly, between the United States and the Soviet Union. Aimed at preventing Soviet domination of Europe on the one hand and countering Western hostility toward Communism and threats of interference with Soviet internal affairs on the other hand, the two sides quickly built up military establishments designed to deter each other in Europe.

To the West the Warsaw Pact is in a position to threaten a rapid conquest of Europe, with great conventional arms superiority, which could be countered only by early use of tactical nuclear weapons and the threat of an attack on the Soviet Union by strategic weapons. The West has always maintained that its forces are solely defensive in character. I have never been able to ascertain if that is the way the Soviets view them or whether they think of them as threatening.

The Gorbachev proposals for force reductions as well as changes in doctrine, as reported by CISAC's Soviet counterparts, from an offensive to a defensive posture should, if implemented, provide a basis for future serious force reduction and restructuring. If the political climate in the Soviet Union continues to change along the lines we have seen under Mr. Gorbachev's leadership, the question of intention, as compared with capability, will begin to play a more important role. To be slightly facetious about this, we have an enormous capability against Canada, but the Canadians do not seem to be the least bit frightened, because they know our intentions are honorable.

It is, frankly, already unimaginable, to me at least and perhaps to others, that the Warsaw Pact would attack Europe. I think that the grave caution with which we now approach the issues of conventional force stability, with concern over bean counting and verification, is partly a carryover from 20 years of negotiations on strategic systems. More important, there is a great body of military experience and folklore about the principles of conventional warfare that has gone largely unquestioned for far too long. While outsiders have not hesitated to offer advice and criticism on nuclear weapons issues, they have largely accepted the position that the military has been at the problem of nonnuclear war for so long that they must know what they are doing.

This situation seems to be changing. As a consequence of new technologies and, in particular, advances in command, control, communications, and intelligence, it is by no means obvious that, even with the numerical superiorities in some weapons categories, the Warsaw Pact, in fact, would prevail in a conventional war with NATO. It is not written anywhere that you must fight tanks with tanks, and so on. The time seems ripe for some very significant moves that would lessen the likelihood that the forces held by NATO and the Warsaw Pact would be, in fact, unleashed in a crisis. That is what is meant by "crisis stability."

Professor Doty referred to the testimony before the Senate Armed Services Committee, on April 6, 1989, of no less an authority than General Andrew Goodpaster, who made a series of very significant suggestions. This is not a woolly headed academic (though he does have a Ph.D. from Princeton); he is a highly respected military man. The suggestions that he made would have a dramatic impact on stability. For example, as Professor Doty quoted, he proposes a radical restructuring of the forces of NATO and the Warsaw Pact on the basis of parity, with total active forces on each side at no more than 50 percent of NATO strength. Another suggestion: continued U.S. force presence in Western Europe, land and air, but at no more than 50 percent of current values. These are rather heretical suggestions. In another forum I understand he has brought into question a number of other shibboleths that have always been used to support the current NATO force structure, regardless of Soviet actions or intentions.

Professor Meselson talked to us about chemical weapons. There is something extremely unpleasant about chemical weapons. In my own experience, I had an uncle who was gassed during World War I. The fear of their use appeared frequently during World War II. Then there is their actual use in the recent Iran-Iraq war and concern about that lunatic Gadhafi and the so-called pharmaceutical plant kindly provided by the Germans—I hope that is not what Chancellor Kohl meant when he said Germany did not need these weapons anymore.

Compared with nuclear weapons, as Professor Meselson has told us, chemical weapons are sort of "greasy kid's stuff." But under the right circumstances they can be quite devastating, and, of course, they are much more readily accessible than nuclear weapons and are a potential terrorist weapon. At the present time there is great support for the treaty being negotiated at the Chemical Weapons Convention in Geneva, which would, in fact, ban the manufacture, possession, and transfer of chemical weapons and be subject to onsite international verification. There is, as he has pointed out, no international law against production or possession of poison-gas weapons, only the "no first use" agreement of the 1925 protocol.

The last subject discussed today was nuclear proliferation. It has always seemed that a world with more than the current five acknowledged possessors of nuclear weapons is an inherently less stable one. India, of course, has exploded a nuclear device, and I think it is reasonable to presume that it must have some actual weapons. Of course, it strains credulity to believe that Israel does not have nuclear weapons. We heard today about the rumors rampant about Pakistan and South Africa. Incidentally, with regard to developing a nuclear weapons program without testing, I might remind you that the Hiroshima bomb was used without having been tested.

It is vitally important, as Mr. Keeny has emphasized, to maintain the nonproliferation regime that has prevailed for the past 45 years and to strengthen the 1968 treaty in the review of 1990 and again in 1995. Unfortunately, among the 130 current signatories, some of the most likely suspects are not included. But as the United States and the USSR make progress toward START, and perhaps movement toward a comprehensive test ban, they will be in a better moral position to urge smaller nations to eschew nuclear weapons and engage their cooperation in keeping them out of the possession of the truly irresponsible.

Professor Doty noted that the world is spending about $1 trillion a year on arms. This tragic waste of money and the associated productive talent diverted from humane endeavors must be stopped. The resources needed to arrest the physical deterioration of the planet may simply not be available if this international mania is not ended. Overpopulation of the earth, the greenhouse effect, ozone-layer depletion, rain forest and species destruction, drought, hunger, and energy requirements are the things that will provoke the international security issues in the twenty-first century. We must, as a world community, dedicate ourselves to survival, and no time, no money, and no resources can be wasted.